All the Families of the Earth

All the Families of the Earth

Therapists in Bible Times

BARBARA LAYMON

foreword by Scotty Hargrove

RESOURCE *Publications* • Eugene, Oregon

ALL THE FAMILIES OF THE EARTH
Therapists in Bible Times

Resource Publications
An Imprint of Wipf and Stock Publishers
199 W. 8th Ave., Suite 3
Eugene, OR 97401

www.wipfandstock.com

PAPERBACK ISBN: 978-1-6667-8308-7
HARDCOVER ISBN: 978-1-6667-8309-4
EBOOK ISBN: 978-1-6667-8310-0

VERSION NUMBER 10/03/23

I dedicate this book to
Linda Dwyer, family systems therapist, and to family
therapists and pastoral counselors everywhere.

Te totum applica ad textum;
rem totam applica ad te.

Apply your whole self to the text;
Apply it all to yourself.

J. A. BENGEL, 1734

Contents

Family Charts

Foreword

THE STORIES THAT MAKE up family life give us a critically important understanding of ourselves and the environment in which we grow up and live. Keeping up with those families, learning from them, and staying in touch with them are rich sources of satisfaction and growth for both individuals and family units over time.

Biblical stories offer similar if not the same opportunities to learn and profit from the wisdom of the Scriptures. Barbara Laymon brings her knowledge and experience in Bowen family systems theory and her grounding in Judeo-Christian thought to shine a bright beam on these familiar stories to highlight important processes that underscore the historical truths that they contain.

Rooted in the science that undergirds Bowen theory, she offers intimate perspectives of the personalities and behavior of the various biblical characters that give a rich understanding of the intergenerational processes that are so important in a mature, realistic appreciation of biblical literature. Without getting too much into the inner workings of the theory, she makes maximum use of it to get to the meaning of Scripture.

This volume offers two important opportunities for the person who seeks to understand Scripture. First, ministers who want to proclaim the truth of Scripture will find fresh insight into its meaning. The similarities of the struggles of biblical characters to those of modern families are clear in Laymon's presentation. Those similarities offer useful homiletical opportunities to clarify biblical meaning to modern people, particularly to families.

Second, people who struggle to find meaning in their own lives will discover that the principles of Bowen theory offer a vehicle for relevant explanation of biblical stores and their own anxiety and turbulence. Bowen's basis in the science of human behavior gives an undeniable reality to the dynamics of modern families that are essentially the same as those in biblical times.

This volume also provides guidance in biblically based preaching and counseling for pastors, priests, and others who are involved in relating the meaning of religious life to the everyday lives of families that experience a wide range of struggles.

Scotty Hargrove, PhD

Preface

WHEN LIFE GETS HARD, as it tends to do, we often look to others for wisdom and perspective. My guess is that the people in the Bible also sought counsel whenever tension was high. Here, I imagine therapists behind the scenes of Scripture.

I've started with the biblical record and expanded on the human side of the narrative. I've simplified a few theological complexities, such as the Bible's various titles for God, choosing to use *the* LORD throughout. I've worked to avoid anachronisms, although some—such as the ability to journal—have seemed necessary. In short, I've interpreted Scripture from a particular counseling perspective: a family systems therapy lens.

I believe that family systems concepts—ideas like facing challenges, connecting with others, managing one's own anxiety, seeing all sides of a situation, and keeping one's principles and goals in mind—have always been not only part of the repertoire of human behavior but also, well, wise. Wisdom itself is nothing new. It all begins with knowing oneself, and, from my perspective, that begins with knowing one's family.

Murray Bowen, who developed family systems theory, sought to understand emotional illness in the context of the natural world. He insisted on clear vocabulary for formulating a science of human behavior. I'm also a believer in straightforward language. My effort here is to use nontechnical terms to describe human emotional processes within, between, and among people. Any and all errors—regarding family systems theory or Scripture or both—are entirely my own.

Families are messy. People make mistakes. The Scriptures, often with painful clarity, record just how imperfect we are. I have written this book for anyone who has ever tried to use the Bible to make sense of our species and what we are doing here on earth.

The last entry of each chapter provides charts, comments, and questions, inviting readers to think alongside the therapists about the families of Scripture. In the appendix, I provide overall guidelines for small group discussion and an online resource for further information. I am interested in what you, the reader, find useful (or not). For me, the family systems framework has provided new ways to think about biblical families.

Acknowledgments

How far back does the journey of a book begin? With this one, several thousand years, anyhow, when Abram and Sarai started out to find a new home. The people who told and retold their story, the people who recorded their story on scrolls, the people who preserved the Scriptures—I am indebted to them all.

My own family story, replete with people who worked to improve the lot of the next generation, includes a dedication to assuring that the children knew both the principles of faith and congregational life. Without such an upbringing, without church community and friendships of faith along the way, my life would have been infinitely poorer. I am indebted to all.

About midway through my life, I began seeing a family systems therapist. And I started writing what would become, in 2004, my first book. Friends listened patiently through the challenges of each step. To describe my path to becoming a writer, though, I must go back to an advanced composition professor at Furman University, Duncan McArthur. Or do I go back to my childhood, to the childless couple up the street who gave me a hardbound copy of *Little Women*, which I still have on my bookshelf?

Back to the present, Marcia Ford, the freelance editor for an early version of this book, helped me to find my footing here. Keith G. Lopes sharpened my family charts to finished, professional pages. Matt Wimer, managing editor at Wipf and Stock, brought the project to fruition. I am indebted to all.

Some academic influences. First, years ago, I took a few classes at the University of the South. My New Testament Greek professor,

Richard Smith, tuned my ear toward biblical interpretation. My Old Testament professor, Rebecca Wright, provided thoughtful views, then and now. Second, faculty and fellow students in the pastoral counseling program of Loyola University Maryland had an influence that continues to shape my professional life. Third, faculty at the Bowen Center for the Study of the Family have, over the past fifteen years, taken considerable time to foster my understanding of family systems theory. Colleagues and clients have been my teachers as well. I am indebted to all.

Finally, many family members served as thought partners while I pondered beliefs articulated in this book. Recently, my cousin's monthly Zoom call gave me a place to consider how to approach different topics. Our children, their spouses, and now, our grandchildren, with their unbridled affection for me, gave me energy for writing. I am indebted to all.

Lastly, my husband. His perhaps unenviable position as my first editor, in writing and in life, has brought out my best thinking here. I am forever indebted to him for our life together.

Introduction

RECENTLY, I RECEIVED A set of journals dating back thousands of years. How they came to me—in print form, no less—is a long story that I will spare you. What they include, though, is short and simple: the diary entries of those who counseled biblical characters.

When working with a counselor or a therapist or a coach or a consultant, there are two possible errors. The first is to discount everything they say, as though they have nothing to offer. The second is to hang onto their every word, as though they know it all. The middle way—to use them as thought partners in seeking truth—is the challenge.

With that warning, let us turn to the journals. To organize the material, which had a dating system beyond my comprehension, I numbered and named the journal entries, listing the corresponding Bible reading as best I could. Much can be gained by following the complete story in the Bible itself; I recommend a careful read (and multiple translations) whenever possible.

For now, let's begin. A flawed and entirely human young woman named Emma is the first journal keeper. To her credit, she is a devoted diarist.

1

In Beginning

Entry 1.1

Emma

Gen 12:1–2

Dear Diary,

Yes, I've started a new page. We've left home, on a journey with Sarai and Abram to find another place to live. Sarai said *the* LORD told Abram to move to a new land. Who is the LORD? I don't know. What new land? Well, that's still to be revealed too.

Who came with us? I do know the answer to this one. Remember my Uncle Micah? The one I liked so much when I was little? He's my great-uncle, a cousin of Sarai's. If he hadn't come, I doubt that the rest of our family would be here at all.

Don't get me wrong, I've been through worse. It's just that we—Uncle Micah's people, basically—are good at a few things but *not* at herding and foraging, which seem to be all that's needed now. Some of us are handy. We can turn clay into a pot or a cave into a home. We know how to keep beehives. Maybe someday our skills will be needed again, but for now, we seem altogether useless. Except for the Seekers.

The Seekers? My mother used to call them that. She said that not only do they seek to understand life, but also others seek them out—for wisdom to get them through their troubles. The Seekers include Micah and a few others who have joined him in the work. Mother even went to Micah for help once herself, when something had happened, I don't remember what. I wonder what she would say if she were here. She might chuckle, but she might be pleased.

Because you see, Diary, yesterday Micah asked me (me!) whether I would be interested in doing the work that the Seekers do. First, I laughed. A nervous laugh, I admit. Well, he didn't laugh, or even smile, which made it worse. "Umm . . . Uncle Micah, why would anyone come to me for wisdom?" I asked.

"Who said anything about wisdom, Emma," he said, grinning. I relaxed a bit as he explained that people come to talk when they are afraid, or worried. That Seekers are wise to the extent that they are humble, refusing to give advice, refraining from judging others.

I tilted my head and frowned too. Inside, I was thinking that while I may be young and newly married and childless, I'm not dumb. "There's got to be more to it than that," I said.

He smiled. "Well, I do put in a few good questions, every once in a while." He thought for a minute, and then he said, "You seem interested in others. You tend to listen and try to understand how they see things. That's something. That's all I'm looking for."

So okay. Leaving aside the wisdom piece, and thank goodness that's not a requirement, I'm thinking, he's right, I do listen. I try to understand what others are thinking. Doesn't everybody? I guess not, now that I think about it. And I am interested right down to my toes. Could this work be for me?

Your hopeful diarist,
Emma

Entry 1.2
Seekers
Gen 12:3

Dear Diary,

Yesterday Micah brought together all the Seekers—those who have been counseling others for years—and people like me, newly invited to the work. He started with questions: How do families bless their member/diarists? What would it take to bless all the families of the earth? People talked about the responsibilities of families and how they often work well together. "Like bees," Micah said, thinking aloud.

The Seekers seemed to wonder about everything. Some are serious questions. "How do families shape individuals into the persons they become?" Some are funny. "What's the help that helps?" Good thing I didn't laugh at that one, for they had quite the conversation about what can get in the way of a person who asks for counsel. I wasn't following all of it, but I did see how some anxiety (prompted by a challenge or difficulty) is necessary for a person to grow up.

They drew a lot of triangles. No, not for gazing at the stars, nor for making music, and we weren't building any pyramids either. These were sets of three people, showing how the individuals relate to each other. In some triangles, one of the three people remains on the outside most of the time, and the other two draw close together. In others, everyone is more equally connected, with more flexibility to move to an inside or outside position, as needed. Triangles can form and shift depending on the circumstances. In large families, there are many interlocking triangles. It made sense to me at the time, and I was intrigued.

Then I started doubting myself. Micah noticed how quiet I was, and when he took me aside, I told him that I couldn't quite imagine becoming a Seeker. "What would I say? Who would be interested in talking to me?" I asked.

"Thinking with people while they figure out their lives is full of surprises," he said. "You have to be ready for that. It is not easy.

But the fact that you're considered insignificant—a young wife—will be a good thing. People are more likely to talk openly to the less 'important' among us."

"There has to be some advantage to my small place in the world," I said, with a small, sad smile.

"What helps you reflect on your life? What gives you perspective?" he asked, ignoring my hint of helplessness.

I saw that he was leaving the decision up to me. And I knew what would help me to decide. This morning, I headed to a cave where I like to go to think. It's a lovely spot, high on the side of a mountain ridge, with a view that goes on forever, and protection from the wind and the rain and the dust and the heat and the cold. Maybe it would be a good place to talk with anyone who wants to see me. Maybe the calm and hope that I have when I'm there would spread to them. Maybe if I could be the person I'm trying to become, they could too. Maybe.

I'm thinking, I will try. If my mother found it useful to go to a Seeker, that's enough. I know she would want me to try. If I can't do it, I will know that soon enough too.

Your bit more realistic diarist,

Emma

Entry 1.3
First couple
Gen 12:4–7

Dear Diary,

Today Abram and Sarai came to see me. I already knew their problem, of course, everyone does. Sarai cannot get pregnant, plain and simple. I asked them what they thought about our current circumstances. Would all the traveling we've been doing have anything to do with their inability to have children?

Abram launched into a whole story about how the LORD had told them to move and had promised them offspring. I asked Sarai what she thought about the LORD's promise that they would have a child, and she kind of laughed—snorted. Then Abram got mad, blaming her. Then she started crying and blaming him for their problems. Their voices were getting louder and the whole conversation was falling apart and I was thinking, *oh no, what am I going to do*, when I remembered to ask them to talk to me instead of to each other.

Yes, you heard me right. They are sitting right next to each other, but they each talk only to me. This is one of Micah's big ideas. When partners can watch each other talking to a third person, they have a chance to notice what's happening within their own selves. By observing their *own* reactions, they are less tangled up together and less focused on what the other should do. Each starts to see their own options.

Today, what came up was their sense of loneliness, of isolation. Isolated? Yes, I know, a bunch of us are around. But think of the people they've lost. Abram's father just died in Haran. His brother died earlier, before we left Ur. Sarai? Well, many of her family members stayed in Ur (not that I blame them, what a great town!). At any rate, she's got her cousin (my great-uncle Micah) and his family, but not a lot of others she's close to. So yeah, in our travels, they've left a lot of family and friends behind.

In my mind, things were starting to make sense. Does loneliness make a person more anxious? And less likely to conceive?

Maybe it's not just their age. I wonder, if Sarai's mother were around, would Sarai be calmer about having a baby?

Abram said the isolation bothers him less. He said he's not lonely, as he always has the LORD with him. I admit, I was surprised. I never thought he really *believed* in the LORD. I always thought the LORD story was his way of getting people to join them in the move away from Haran.

While I was trying to look interested in what he was saying about the LORD, inside I was scrambling for what to say next. I mean, a vision about a cosmic being telling an older man that his older wife is going to have a baby is a tad strange, right? What had Micah taught us about reality-based thoughts?

He is the head of our tribe, of course. And sometimes people are attracted to leaders who lean toward supernatural explanations. Nothing like telling people that such-and-such a god will solve all of our problems.

What do I believe? At least around here, people worship multiple gods—one for too little rain, one for too much rain, one for health, one for the sheep, you name it. A person could go crazy trying to please all of them. It is not for me. But to give Abram credit, when I listen to him talk about the LORD, I hear something else. His loyalty to the LORD is a part of who he is.

The supernatural, though, that's not my area. My job here is to keep Abram and Sarai focused on how they see the real challenges of life. The chance that they will have a baby is a possibility still in the mix, even though they don't seem to take much stock in it.

Your learning-in-action diarist,
Emma

Entry 1.4
Anxious Abram
Gen 12:10–15

Dear Diary,

Abram came to see me by himself today. The reason? You'll never guess. There's been a famine, and we've been traveling down to Egypt to find food. On the way, Abram got worried that the Egyptians would kill him so that they could have Sarai, beautiful Sarai.

Listen, though, to his solution. He avoided any mention of Sarai being his wife, and instead told the Egyptians that *she was his sister*. Then, Pharaoh's people swooped in and took Sarai back to Pharaoh's household.

I thought, well, Sarai is lovely, but really? Sure, she does look younger than her years. But it is not like there are no pretty women in all of Egypt, nor a way to hide or disguise her. Then I started wondering what's happening to her, in Pharaoh's house, alone. How is Sarai being treated now? Is she safe? For a minute, I did not know what to do with my fears for her nor what to say to Abram.

I did know what I was thinking: What a jerk! Then I caught myself. It's one of Micah's big ideas: no judging, stay neutral, never take sides. I know, that's three ideas. Anyhow, staying detached is the most important thing I can do. I knew enough to stop heading down the path I was on, but how? How might I pull myself together and find a fresh curiosity about his views? What could I say next?

My mind went to my sister's children, who occasionally say something that either I don't quite follow or that leaves me speechless. I've learned to repeat a few of their words back to them. Usually they have more to say, and it gives me a minute to collect my thoughts and to understand theirs. "You think Sarai is beautiful," I said.

Jackpot. He must have talked for ten minutes. He said that of course she is beautiful, without question, and that her beauty creates real problems for him. In his mind, everyone wants to sleep with Sarai. Further, his life is at risk anytime a foreign, able-bodied man is around—for anyone (outside our tribe) might kill him to have her. He is *that anxious.*

So, this is how he sees it! What a relief, once I understood. I always thought that Sarai was the worrier, but he is one anxious Abe, and the anxiety may be keeping him from thinking clearly. I don't know for sure, and the idea needs more exploring with him. Still, I wonder if something about his family set him up to be extra vigilant about what could go wrong. In his family, did he function as the one on the alert for any potential threat, realistic or not?

I wondered what Abram's mother was like. Did she raise him to think that his needs always came first? That he could count on her to give up herself for him? If so, then it would be automatic for him to think that Sarai wouldn't mind being taken, if it met his need to stay calm about his own life.

Then I started to catch on to the bigger picture. Sarai's willingness to go along with whatever Abram decides to do—including lending her to Pharaoh—not only keeps him stuck, behaving like a child, but also continues her own tendency (which she must have grown up with?) to give up herself for others. They are a perfect fit for each other. The idea that they are in it together helped me to think more clearly, with more neutrality. The sun was setting, though, and it was time to stop.

Your less-mad-at-Abram diarist,

Emma

Entry 1.5

Deceit

Gen 12:16–20; 20:12

Dear Diary,

When Abram came today, he had Sarai with him. I was so relieved to see them both, I had to take a minute to breathe. So much for neutrality, right? I've been thinking, though, that while I want to avoid judging Abram or anyone else, I'm not aiming to be so neutral that I don't care what happens to them. What am I trying for? I want to be indifferent, respectful, to leave to others what is theirs to decide. I can't fake it—indifference, that is—I must let go of feeling responsible for others. How do I get there? One clue I've discovered. When I can notice my feelings, without getting caught up in them, indifference seems more possible.

Sarai seemed no worse for the wear. She reported that Pharaoh and his household had been sick the entire time she had been with them—she alone had stayed healthy. Pharaoh eventually connected the household sickness to her presence. He confronted Abram, demanding to know why he had been deceived. Why had Abram failed to mention that he was married to Sarai and called her his sister? "Here is your wife, take her, and be gone," Pharaoh said, his last words to Abram.

Sarai and Abram were both laughing as though it were a childish prank, reminding me of their equal immaturity. Where do I go next? Sometimes, my job is to lighten the conversation, so that people can think more clearly. Other times, like today, it's to get more serious.

I tried to evoke a new perspective by asking what else had happened between each of them and Pharaoh. Sarai said her contact with him had been very limited. Abram said that Pharaoh had given him many gifts—livestock and enslaved people, both male and female. They got quieter as they considered the facts.

Then I asked Abram what the LORD had said to him about all of this. He looked surprised at the question. He sat up a little straighter and finally said that he and the LORD had not talked about it. He seemed distracted by the question and had little more to say.

Sarai and I started talking about the story that she was half-sister to Abram. Sarai was certain that she and Abram had different mothers. She had no memory of her father at all. So that conversation went nowhere.

I do wonder about her childhood, Diary, and how hard it is for her to talk about the past. As an adult, she has moved far away from most of her relatives. What difference has her lack of family connection made in her life? Did my Uncle Micah bring us along on this journey, knowing that Sarai needed some kinfolk with her?

Wondering,
Emma

Entry 1.6
New worries
Gen 13:1–9

Dear Diary,

Abram and Sarai came in today with new worries. Always more chaos in their lives, that's for sure. Today's problem involved the increasing sizes of the flocks of Abram and his nephew Lot. I thought it was funny at first—Pharaoh's last laugh, giving Abram so much livestock that now, added to the existing flocks and herds, the situation has become unmanageable.

Then I realized that they were not laughing. What's the trouble? Well, besides the actual difficulty around finding enough water for all the sheep, the tension between Abram's herders and Lot's herders is growing, with each group blaming the other for the problem. Also, Sarai said that the more time Abram spends working with Lot, the more she feels left out. Abram has proposed that he and Lot split up—Lot will go in one direction, and he'll take the other.

Abram and Sarai both think that not having Lot around will make things better. The more they talked about it, the more concerned I got. Aren't there other solutions to the problem besides the family splitting up? Do we really need so many flocks? What's going to happen without Lot around? He is a relatively young man, after all, and he is a useful member of our group. We talked for a long time but got nowhere.

Your perplexed diarist,
Emma

Entry 1.7
Seeking advice
Gen 13:8–13

Dear Diary,

I heard the news this morning that Abram and Lot have already split up. Lot picked the well-watered plain of Jordan. Not only that, but I've also heard that he is moving his tent all the way to Sodom, a town with a bad reputation.

It has made me think about my last session with Abram and Sarai. I wish I could have done a better job with it. They thought they had a simple problem, one that involved land for grazing sheep, but I doubt it. I think something else was and is happening, although I cannot put my finger on it. It might be a good question to take to the Council.

What is the Council? It's going to sound odd, but we—all of us Seekers, old and young, experienced, or not, all of us—sit down together to talk about the work we do. Each time we meet, one person reports, sketching out a family chart and providing some facts of the situation. Then she or he explains her main questions and concerns.

And then, others—usually, the more senior individuals—respond with *their* ideas. Each person gives their perspective, usually beginning with a couple of comments on how they are thinking. They get clear about the problem at hand and then they ask some questions.

It's a little odd, but it works. Questions help me catch on more than explanations—and catch on to myself, on what is getting in my way. Asking good questions is not an easy business, and I listen carefully for how it is done. The idea is to frame things up without blaming anyone or leading anyone towards a specific answer. *Who* asks *what* doesn't matter—it's the questions that can give some new perspective. I'll write them down so that I can keep thinking about them later.

This will be my first time to share my work, and I'm more than a little nervous. Nothing like the chance to show how little

I know. Oh well, right? Everyone says how useful it is, how much the different perspectives help them to see the family more clearly. And I can already say that every time the Council meets, I get a little more understanding.

I'm going to go ahead and prepare for it, putting in the family chart, family facts, and the questions and ideas I want to talk about. When the Council meets, I will keep a list of their comments: thoughts, questions, and ideas. And I'm going to try to put the comments into categories by topic. I think it's time to start naming them. If Micah wants to think about how these ideas apply in all families and maybe all living things, having names for the concepts would be a start.

Fingers crossed for tomorrow,
Emma

Entry 1.8
Seekers' Council—Emma, presenter
Gen 11:27—12:1

Introduction

I appreciate the chance to present here at the Council. I have been working with Abram and Sarai since we left Haran. I've seen them as a couple and in separate, individual sessions.

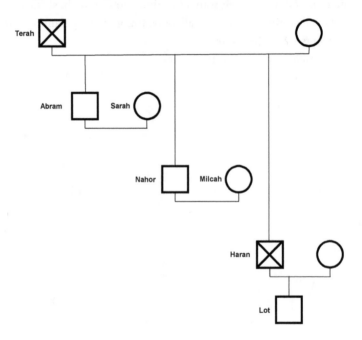

Figure 1. Abram's family. **Terah and his wife, whose name is unknown, had three sons. Abram was the oldest, with two younger brothers—Nahor and Haran. Haran died in Ur, leaving a son, Lot. After Haran's death (noted by the *x* in the figure), the multigenerational family moved on. They had intended to go to Canaan but settled in a town that was also named Haran. After Terah died, Abram and Sarai left Haran for Canaan, taking Lot with them.**

Concerns and questions

Abram, Sarai, and Lot have been together for a long time. In the time I've worked with them, Abram and Sarai have complained about Lot more and more lately. The tension among the three of them has been clear. Add to that the tension among Abram's and Lot's herders. Did tension keep them from working together to solve their problems? If they could have gotten along, would the size of their herds have become a more manageable problem? How could I have opened up a different way of looking at the situation? I wonder how I might have been more useful to the family.

Council comments by topic

1. Individuality and togetherness

Emma, people seem to be pulled two ways. On the one hand, each person wants to be his or her own person. On the other hand, everyone wants to be together with others. It might sound easy—that families can both stay connected and respect one another as separate individuals—but, as this family problem shows, it is difficult to do. When people start feeling the pressure of too much togetherness, with too much emphasis on pleasing others, then they are going to find ways to distance from each other. Either that, or they have to grow up a bit, finding ways to manage themselves around each other, without losing who they are in the meantime.

Given what we know about the family of Abram and Lot, I'd say their separation was predictable. Going forward, will they find ways to stay in touch? To relate to each other, as two adults?

2. Tension

It's interesting how tension between Lot's and Abram's herders was part of the situation. I wonder if the tension began with them, and spread to Lot and Abram, or if it went the other way, from Lot and Abram down to the herders? Did blame go back and forth, with increased intensity, decreasing the capacity to think logically, to consider other solutions? Were they looking for an excuse to distance? In other words, was it an emotional decision with a rational-sounding basis, that the sheep needed more room to graze?

In my view, managing tension by distancing is a tried-and-true method for calming things down for a bit. Over the long run, though, distancing is a temporary solution at best, as it decreases overall resourcefulness. The loss of connection means a reduced ability to solve problems, on both sides, with a loss of knowledge, connections, and skill.

3. Focus on a child

Another method that couples often use to manage tension is to focus on a third person, often a child, who learns, over time, to expect it. The focus can be positive or negative. What made Abram and Sarai decide to bring Lot along, when they left Ur? How has the focus on Lot become a way to channel the family's anxiety? Will their marriage become even more intense without Lot there?

4. Triangles

I like to use triangles in my work. They are everywhere—when two people have any tension, they add a third. It's as predictable as the sun coming up in the morning. Noticing how anxiety moves around a family, through the triangles within it, has been a huge help to me.

How does the triangle operate between Abram, Sarai, and Lot? Did it begin with Sarai on the outside, and a closeness of working together between Abram and Lot? And then the tension over the grazing of the animals, between Abram and Lot, allowed Sarai to move to the inside, with Abram?

5. Family patterns over time

Emma, I heard your question about what you might have done or said differently. It's always important to consider, of course, although it is easy to overestimate our influence. Real change happens slowly. I'm wondering to what extent these family patterns might have been in place for many generations. For instance, was Lot's dad also the one everyone worried about, before Lot was ever born? Is it a family tradition, that they focus on a child? Lot's father was a youngest—a sibling position that can invite a focus, you see.

More generally, though, if these patterns are ever going to change, might anxiety be a necessary first step? Will anxiety in the family unit continue to increase? Time will tell.

2

Complications

Dear Diary,

As usual, Sarai and Abram came in today with a lot on their minds. First, they wanted to talk about Lot, who has already gotten into trouble in Sodom. Abram had to put together a small army to go rescue him! They were moaning and groaning, putting the focus right back on Lot, even though he's moved away.

All this came with some comfortable joining between the two of them. How two people can make peace at the expense of a third! They agreed that Lot was in over his head and they had to save him once again, and so on and so forth, on and on. Boring. I could not figure out a way to interrupt them, and I must admit that I lost track of the conversation for a minute there.

Then, out of nowhere, Sarai made a demand. She has to have a baby. She does not care how it happens, only that she must have one. The disrespect she is shown as a childless woman must stop, and right now, she said. I tried to explore her thoughts and feelings, but she was having none of that. Her idea is that Abram should provide them with a child by getting Hagar pregnant.

Who is Hagar? She is an enslaved person, one that we took away from Egypt, and she works as Sarai's maid. If Sarai arranges for Hagar to have Abram's baby, then Sarai saves face.

Well, that idea woke me up. Abram indicated with some solemnity that he felt he should do Sarai's bidding. Eye roll, right? I mean, Hagar is maybe fifteen years old—young, alone, and attractive. Sarai, for her part, seemed to be looking forward to the new sleeping arrangements.

I knew *something* would happen when Lot left, but *this* had not occurred to me. It seemed that neither of them had thought the idea through. I tried to engage them in some questions about how the decision might change their lives.

I asked about the chance that she and Abram might still have a baby. What might happen to her offspring if Hagar had a son first—a son who, as the older, would inherit everything? She shrugged, reminding me that it was not my job to think for her. If she can't imagine it, she can't hear it from me.

I went in another direction, asking Sarai what her mother would say about the idea, if she were still alive. Well, that went nowhere too. Sarai avoids *any* talk about her mother, and I was reminded of how useful it might be to spend some time talking with her about their relationship. Getting to know parents as ordinary human beings—neither sainted nor despised—is part of growing up. There are a lot of ways to work on it, even if the parents are no longer living.

But it was not the moment for that conversation. I turned to Abram, asking what he thought. He started a story about his descendants and the LORD telling him to count the stars in the sky. Mid-story, he got uneasy and changed the subject. I knew better than to press him. The whole session was a confusing mess.

In the end, all I got from each of them was a sense of urgency about Abram's having a baby with someone, anyone. I wonder what I could have done differently. How could I have prompted more thoughtfulness? They could not bring themselves to reflect on the pressure they were feeling to have a baby or to consider the consequences of their actions. It is a less than ideal way to decide something, that's for sure.

Your one surprised diarist,

Emma

Entry 2.2
Finding the mature side
Gen 16:1–14

Dear Diary,

Remember a while back when I was thinking that Abram was a jerk? You know, when he hid his marriage to Sarai to protect himself from Pharaoh? Well, come to find out, Sarai is an equal jerk.

What happened? First, Sarai gave Hagar to Abram as a wife. And once Hagar was pregnant, tension between the two women began. Sarai said that being around Hagar, watching Hagar carrying Abram's baby, made her feel even more ashamed of her own childlessness. Of course, Abram (the spineless, when it comes to his homelife) told Sarai that Hagar was her slave-girl—without mentioning that she was also his wife—and to do whatever she pleased with her.

I could see Sarai's side of it, how the shame of childlessness had overwhelmed her. But when she started describing how harshly she was treating Hagar for her "bad behavior," I almost lost it. Apparently, it got so bad that Hagar ran away. That's desperate, for there is nothing but wilderness around us, on every side.

Hagar did come back and I've heard it said that an angel of the LORD told her to return. If so, the LORD has spoken to two people I know. Abraham and Hagar—two more different people, in age, gender, and position in the tribe I cannot imagine. What do they have in common? What does this say about the LORD?

Back to Sarai, though. Sarai said that she continues to feel less of a person, anytime Hagar is around. Whenever she sees Hagar's pregnant body, she gets upset. Pulling myself together, I saw the task of the hour. For Hagar and her unborn child to have a chance, Sarai would need to find a bigger perspective. I went with the emotions first, asking Sarai what choices she has. Does she have to accept this feeling of shame? Could she decide for herself whether she had anything to be ashamed of? Can anyone or anything make us feel a certain way, unless we allow it? Well, Diary, I'm going to have to work on how to ask that. Maybe not when a person is upset, for sure. It went nowhere.

I switched to a thinking question, asking Sarai for her best guess about Hagar's chances of having a healthy baby. Hagar was young, I reasoned. What had Sarai noticed about the chances of a young woman like Hagar having a child who was born early, or underweight, or stillborn?

Sarai had a ready answer for this one. She's watched other women having babies for many years, with careful attention. Sometimes, she observed, a mother of any age can have a small or sickly baby. Other times, during a famine or drought, pregnant women all suffer, but especially the youngest ones, and their babies are less likely to make it. She went on for a bit about the best foods and herbs during pregnancy.

Then she sighed. "I see," she said. "Hagar's child must be born healthy. That's all that matters now. Still, I can hardly stand to be around her these days. She has everything I have ever wanted."

We talked about feelings and the capacity to reason with one's emotions. What can one do with envy or feeling disrespected? When is it possible to notice an emotion and attend to it, without letting it do harm to others? How can one care less about feeling disrespected and more about self-respect? How can one care less about what others think and more about what oneself thinks? All good questions, we decided, with no easy answers.

Speaking of not being easy. Seeing people at their absolute worst and remembering what they are up against is hard, at least for me. I am completely out of energy.

Your worn-out diarist,

Emma

Entry 2.3
Update
Gen 16:9–11, 15–16

Dear Diary,

Last time I wrote to you, I thought I was tired from the session with Sarai. Well, maybe, but it was more than that. I was (am) pregnant. I am sleepy all the time these days. But I wanted to tell you that Hagar has had a healthy baby boy. They named him Ishmael.

Your diarist with child,

Emma

Entry 2.4
Laughter
Gen 17:1–8, 15—18:15

Dear Diary,

So much to catch up on. Yes, I am fine. I have missed writing to you, but the children had to come first for a while. Oh yes, they are fine, growing, and all is well. Hagar's baby boy is no longer a child either. He's thirteen, can you believe it?

Today I met with Abram and Sarai, who told me that they have changed their names to Abraham and Sarah, after the LORD, according to Abraham, renamed them both. Next, Abraham told me that the LORD had promised him (age one hundred) and Sarah (age ninety) a child, a child whom Sarah would conceive and bear. For a second there, I started worrying again about Abraham's grasp on reality. Then he said that he fell on his face and laughed when the LORD made the promise, so I let go of that worry. His capacity to hear the LORD, whoever the LORD is to him, and at the same time to stay grounded, is what matters.

Sarah piped up and said that recently, while entertaining some mysterious travelers who had predicted her having a baby, she had laughed out loud too. The lightness, the humor, is a real change for them. Their relationship, these days, seems less intense and more fun.

Maybe Ishmael's presence has made a difference over these years. Maybe it's taken some of the stress from them as a couple? I'm starting to wonder if they might have a child now. For all I know, thinking that they are *too* old is a good thing—allowing them to relax a little, to quit trying so hard. And then Sarah might just get pregnant. Who knows, right?

I've seen it with my friends. Those who fail to conceive are those who want a baby desperately—and those who get pregnant right away are those who had hardly thought about the possibility. So I responded that they certainly looked old to me, and then they both laughed again!

Your slightly giddy diarist,

Emma

Entry 2.5
A deeper view
Gen 18:22–33

Dear Diary,

Abraham came by himself today—saying that Sarah was a little queasy this morning. He launched into this whole story about Lot, who still occupies his mind. Anyhow, this time it is serious.

Things in Sodom, where Lot settled, and Gomorrah, nearby, have gotten much worse. Now the LORD is threatening to destroy both towns altogether. Abraham reported a whole conversation, asking for wiggle room, so to speak, if righteous people were found in those towns. He politely bargained the LORD down from fifty to forty-five to forty to thirty to twenty to only ten righteous people needed to save the towns.

Well. I decided that it was time to explore his view of the LORD a bit. I was genuinely interested, and I think he could tell. "What's it like, bargaining with a cosmic being?" I asked.

"Well, I wondered if maybe I had heard the LORD wrong the first time," he said. "I mean, would he really sweep away everyone, the good and the bad? It took a lot of back and forth to understand."

"Prayer, in a word? I mean, would you call it that?" I asked.

Abraham sat for a minute. "Not exactly. Maybe, I guess. I would not have put it that way. Sometimes, we have very ordinary conversations, really."

"Well, maybe to you, they are ordinary. Not for me, though, or anyone I've ever talked with," I said.

"Yes, I see," Abraham said. "I can't describe it very well. I get interested in what the LORD is saying. I keep asking questions until I understand. That's all."

We talked some about Lot and his family. Then we talked about life in Sodom and Gomorrah and the destruction that the LORD has threatened there. Abraham reflected on the promises he had made to keep his nephew Lot safe, promises he had made long ago to Lot's father, Haran. Looking back, I think that I had failed—until today—to understand the significance of Abraham's relationship with his younger brother, and how his nephew Lot became so important to him when Haran died.

Your starting-to-see diarist,

Emma

Entry 2.6
Seekers' Council—Emma, presenter
Gen 19:15–38

Introduction

The news about Lot and his family traveled fast. It's such a tough story, I asked for the Council's time right away. Lot and his wife and daughters escaped from Sodom as Sodom and Gomorrah were being destroyed. Lot's wife died as they fled. Lot had originally planned to live in Zoar but was afraid of the people there, so he and his daughters settled in a cave in a more remote area. While living there, Lot's daughters became pregnant by their father.

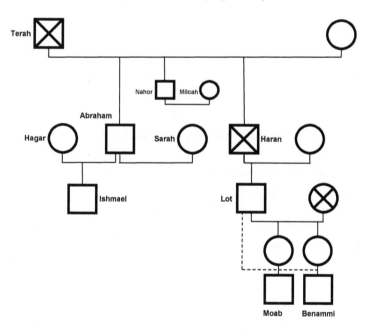

Figure 2. Abraham's family. The family chart shows three recent births. Hagar and Abraham had a son, Ishmael. The dotted lines represent the coupling between Lot and each of his daughters. Each of his daughters had a son, Moab and Benami. The chart also shows two untimely deaths. Lot's father, Haran, died when Lot was a child. His wife died as the family fled Sodom.

Concerns and questions

A few things stand out for me. I'm shocked by what happened and I have noticed in myself a sense of repulsion over the incest between Lot and each of his daughters. I must pull myself together before I talk with Abraham and Sarah. I have worked on neutrality before, but it seems a much more difficult goal this time.

Given the time and energy Abraham and Sarah have put into Lot's life over many years, combined with the promise Abram made to his brother to care for Lot all those years ago, how will they manage their own feelings around what has happened? How can I be useful to them?

Council comments by topic

1. Getting clear

Emma, the feeling of repulsion is an interesting one. Being repulsed by smells, for instance, can keep people from ingesting foods or drinks that might make them sick. Perhaps it is useful to have the response you are describing—useful for families, that is. An instinct to avoid inbreeding, maybe that's a good thing. However, when might a sense of repulsion interfere with the ability to think clearly?

Noticing your reactions may give you a better chance of being able to manage them. It also gives you a view of what Abraham and Sarah may be experiencing. How might a consideration of the facts restore their ability to think objectively? Might it be possible for them to stop and reflect on what Lot and his daughters were up against?

2. Tension management

The death of Lot's wife seems important. If she had still been alive, physically present in the cave, would these events have occurred? More than that, would her presence have helped the family think about their options? Had she been an important, calming influence?

Under pressure, the capacity to be thoughtful is reduced. The higher the intensity, the lower the ability to manage oneself. Isolated from the world, did Lot and his daughters lose touch with a realistic view of their circumstances? How can a person notice when feelings are in charge and the ability to reason has been left behind?

I am also wondering about the alcohol use in the family. Were Lot's daughters drinking with their father? Were all three using alcohol to manage their own fears and anxieties? Does alcohol work on the inside in a way that's like distancing from others on the outside? That is, does alcohol create a cutoff between thoughts and feelings?

3. Cutoff

I'm wondering how Lot's family will move on from this. Given that they are already isolated from the rest of us, how will they manage the tensions of life? Who will absorb it now?

Earlier, when Lot had first moved to Sodom and gotten into some difficulty, Abraham came to his rescue. Since Sodom was destroyed, though, there's been no more talk of that. Are Abraham and Lot going to cut off completely from one another?

Cutoff goes way back in our family. Some of us still remember leaving Ur, when Lot was just a boy. And more recently, when we moved from Haran, we left some family members behind. In a way, when Abraham and Lot separated, they were just following an old family pattern. What began as distancing, though, seems to have become a full cutoff.

What gets lost when families part? What happens to their ability to weigh all the options? To look at problems calmly? To be resourceful rather than helpless?

4. Responsibility

Did all this begin with Lot's father's death and Abraham's taking too much responsibility for his nephew? Did Lot never learn to be responsible for himself? In saying this, I do not mean to pin all this on Abraham either. There is a long history here, that's all, and there's more to it than blaming Lot or his daughters. How can one get away from too much cause-and-effect thinking and, instead, look at all the factors that went into a problem?

What is our contribution to the problem? If we—all of us—had stayed more in touch with Lot and his daughters, would things have been different? What are the chances that Lot himself, even now, might become more responsible for himself and for his offspring?

5. Opposites

In my experience, most families have more or less successful branches, which show up over time. Looking at this family chart, it is easy to see the variation. The Terah-Abraham line has taken a different direction than the Terah-Haran line. When Abraham and Lot chose to part ways, they both had plenty of wealth. But they chose very different paths.

Is it possible that the opposite outcomes are tied to each other? Going back to Lot's youth, that the more Abraham worried over and focused on him, the more Lot became the opposite of Abraham? Or maybe, that the more everyone focused on Lot, the more stuck he became, while others became less stuck, experiencing more freedom? That Abraham's success—and the success of all of us, sitting here, for that matter—was built on Lot's decline? There are many questions one could ask. Abraham can learn a lot from what's happened here, and it could make a difference to his family in the future.

3

Close Call

Entry 3.1
Big picture
Gen 1:1—2:4; Job 12:7—8

Dear Diary,

This afternoon I talked with Uncle Micah about my work with Abraham and Sarah. Other than with you, and at the Council discussions, I never talk about the people I'm seeing. Ever. It was such a relief to take my questions to someone more experienced. And Micah did not disappoint me.

Two things stand out. I asked him what he thought about the way Abraham and Sarah could both be such jerks. I told him I didn't like calling them jerks, but what else was there to say? Abraham, out of fear for himself, lets Pharaoh's people take his wife. Sarah treats Hagar too cruelly for words. I do not want to think badly of them, but I am stuck with what I know.

He asked me—calmly, and I should learn from that—how I would describe their levels of maturity. After a minute, I said I would describe them both as immature, just in different ways. He said he'd been noticing that, too, in his work with couples. As he put it, they are so immature that it takes two of them to make one adult!

"I see. I see how little they have to work with. It is where they are," I said, after thinking for a minute.

"Exactly. The more one can see where they are and how they got there—what their parents were up against, for starters—the less inclined one is to take sides or blame anybody. Noticing that you are taking sides is a start," he said.

"The better way is avoiding that tendency altogether, and staying with people in their darkest moments, without blame. When you scorn others, you dishonor yourself. It is not about the other. It is about honoring yourself and your part in your relationships, in all your thoughts about others and all your dealings with them."

"Micah," I said, "The idea of the LORD blessing our people, what do you think about that?" I talked about how skeptical I had been at first, but that getting to know Abraham and his relationship with said LORD had made me wonder. "Could it be?" I asked. "Could a cosmic presence be with us here, as we wander around looking for a home?"

Micah took a minute to answer me. "I don't know the answer to that," he said. "It's an important question. Maybe the LORD is with us, maybe, with all people. Maybe with everything that breathes. Maybe not. I don't know."

It was quiet, so very quiet, for a minute. Then he changed the subject. "What do you think about Sarah getting pregnant?"

I told him how I had noticed their laughter in our sessions. "You don't suppose their getting more relaxed together has anything to do with her pregnancy?" I asked him.

He laughed. "Perhaps you are serving the LORD now."

Well, this was a new thought for me, that's for sure. Micah speculated that maybe the LORD won't act without us—that more is happening in and through us than we might imagine.

"Okay, I can go that far, maybe, with important people in important moments. But all of us? All the time?" I asked.

"If that's the way life works, wouldn't it happen all the time?" he said. He mentioned the story told last night around the fire, the one about the creation in seven days. He wondered whether the idea of individuality and togetherness—being a separate self while staying connected with others—was expressed in everything that was made. "Some processes seem built into life," he said. "After all, from bees to people, all creatures are individuals *and* part of larger groups."

Right now, I'm looking out at a bird's nest on a ledge and wondering about a lot of things. I am no Micah, but I will not let what he's taught me die. It will continue. That much I can guarantee. Even if it's only in this diary, it will live past my life.

Your determined diarist,

Emma

Entry 3.2
Peas in a pod
Gen 21:1–7

Dear Diary,

Abraham and Sarah came in this morning with their new baby, Isaac. Well, Diary, it was fun, just plain fun, to watch them together with the baby. Abraham is completely smitten. I've never seen anything like it. They are stuck together like two peas in a pod. Sarah too. Three peas in a pod? Something like that. Very comfy for now. Sarah nursed him, and when he fell asleep, she laughed. "Who would have said that I would ever nurse a baby!"

It was sweet, but I wondered how all this coziness was going to turn out for the child. I asked how they imagined that Isaac might someday become a separate person from them. Not an easy idea for any new parents, but at least the question is out there.

The baby kept sleeping, so I asked them to talk about their marriage. What had they learned over the years? What mattered to them now? How had things changed since leaving Haran? It was interesting and I think useful to them, to do a backwards look. Then the baby woke up and they were too wrapped up in the child to talk anymore.

Your fascinated diarist,

Emma

Entry 3.3
Problems
Gen 21:8–11

Dear Diary,

Honestly, people love having problems! If life is good, they can't wait to find a new worry to latch onto. It is as though they have a certain amount of anxiety and must have a problem to soak it all up with. What could Sarah and Abraham possibly be worried about? It's Ishmael, this time.

Sarah is unhappy with the idea that there's another child around who could be competition for her baby boy's inheritance. A few days ago, there was a big weaning party for Isaac. I thought it was fun, but I did notice some tension between Sarah and Hagar.

Sarah said that she was watching Ishmael and Isaac playing together when the big brother started teasing the little one. Yes, I know, I have children, and that's what the older siblings do. But add the teasing to the inheritance problem, and it was more than Sarah could stand. She is demanding that Hagar and Ishmael go.

Abraham seems distressed about the whole situation. "I was overjoyed when Ishmael was born," he said. "Isaac, though, even more so. He is my *together child*. I have no other words for it. We are as one. I would do anything to make life good for him."

Well, okay, I thought. Let me see it from his perspective. Parents can be infatuated by a new baby, which makes the constant care that a newborn requires easier to manage. That got me nowhere, though, as Isaac is not a newborn baby now. The infatuation stage should be ending.

Then I thought about how long they had waited to have Isaac. When a child is special in some way—and Isaac certainly fits that description—the parents can hardly think of anything else. Parents can forget themselves, their relationship, and their own life goals. Worse, in the long run, I've never seen it do a child any good. Whether the parents are always adoring or always disapproving or some potent combination of both is immaterial. The child can be crippled for life.

I asked Abraham if a big brother—sometimes a challenging presence—might be good for Isaac. Isaac might be stronger for it. They might become lifelong friends. I added something about overprotectiveness getting in the way of growth. But Sarah and Abraham had these blank looks in their eyes, like *what is she talking about?!*

I guess they are so used to focusing on a child—first Lot, now Isaac—that it's automatic for them. And, after all the years they've waited to have Isaac, it's not a surprise that they should have tunnel vision now.

Your resigned diarist,
Emma

Entry 3.4
Getting real
Gen 21:12–21

Dear Diary,

The very next morning after Abraham and Sarah came to see me, Abraham sent Hagar and Ishmael away. When Micah heard the news, he left right away and somehow—in what I can only describe as a small miracle—managed to find them out in the wilderness. He seemed relieved when he got back, saying that they were going to be all right. Right now, he's organizing some supplies for their journey.

Looking back, it's almost like I could see this coming. But I could not stop it. Families have their own ways of solving their problems. When they are under pressure, it is hard for them to think. That's all. Being able to get clear about what they are trying to do, defining their goals and then sticking with them, is rare. Doing the most expedient thing at the moment is common. That's reality, and it's nobody's fault. Then again, it's everybody's fault.

Your aiming-for-realistic diarist,

Emma

Entry 3.5
Breakthrough
Gen 22:1–19

My dear Diary,

It's been years—maybe a decade or more, with little news to report—but today, I must write. You will never guess what has happened.

Abraham decided to sacrifice Isaac. Yes, you heard me right. Took him to Moriah, up the mountain, built an altar, and laid the wood on it. At the very last moment, a ram appeared, which Abraham sacrificed instead.

He came in by himself today, claiming (can you guess?) that the LORD told him to do this. While he was talking, another event kept coming into my mind. I don't know why, but I kept remembering the time when he was bargaining with the LORD to try to save Sodom. It was so overwhelming that I could hardly think. So, I went with it. "Did you have a conversation with the LORD about sacrificing Isaac, like the time you talked with the LORD about Sodom?"

"No," he answered, slowly.

"How could this be? How could you stand up to the LORD over Sodom and not over your own son? You walked for three days plus, and never talked to the LORD?"

It took a while to sort this out, and started to make sense only when we began talking about Abraham's father. When Abraham was a child, he was somewhat spoiled—not to the extent of Isaac, but still, treated like the princely firstborn. Up to a point. When his father had had enough, he would blow up, issuing directives that had better be followed or else. A certain blind obedience was required at that point, I gathered.

When I asked Abraham whether he thought the LORD was like his father, he laughed. "My dad was just a person. The LORD is the LORD."

"Does the LORD get mad and require blind obedience?" I asked. Abraham sat quietly for a long time. I could see it in his face, how hard he was thinking. For once, I kept still.

And then he said that on the climb up the mountain, he had become aware of his comfortable closeness to Isaac, his *together child*, that the two of them were so close that he did not know where one began and the other ended. And he could remember thinking about how important Isaac had become to him—somehow, he'd had a dawning awareness on that slow climb, *too* important to him. As he reached that conclusion, a ram appeared for the sacrifice.

Eventually we got back to the question about how he could have bargained with the LORD about Sodom but not about his own son. Abraham said that he could see it now—that he should have tried to understand what the LORD was saying to him. That the LORD did not want him unable to speak, quaking in fear, and rushing to do whatever he'd believed he'd heard without thought or question. That blind obedience is intended for children getting too close to a fire. That the LORD wants the opposite: for him (and Isaac) to grow up. He added that the idea that the LORD would want human sacrifice seems ridiculous now.

It was quite an hour. I expect we'll spend a lot of time reflecting on all he might learn from it. How is the closeness he has with his son getting in his own way? In Isaac's way? And he'll want to think more about his father as a person, to stop endowing him with projections left over from childhood. For now, I can only say that something important happened today.

Your amazed diarist,

Emma

Entry 3.6
Moving the family forward
Gen 22:9–14

Dear Diary,

When Abraham and Sarah walked in today, Sarah looked distinctly older. My cave has a nice warm spot near a gap between the rocks, and I helped her to get comfortable there. Even with help, she had trouble sitting down and getting back up again. She was still Sarah, though, and she was hopping mad.

She began by explaining that the almost-sacrifice of Isaac had happened without her knowledge. Abraham had told her they'd be gone for a few days, exploring some new pastureland for the flocks. And she was already worried about how they were doing, of course, she's always worried about something. When they came back, both father and son were quiet about the whole trip, but once Abraham left, Isaac told her the whole story. Can you imagine? She was beside herself.

Then she ramped it up a notch, saying that she could hear Isaac moaning in his sleep. She's sure he's reliving the moments when he thought he was going to be sacrificed. And it was grisly stuff, as she pointed out—by the time the ram appeared, Abraham had already reached for his knife.

I was trying to think of how to move her beyond the horror of it all. I remembered a tip about how simple, factual questions could sometimes restore an ability to think. So I asked Sarah whether Isaac had ever moaned in his sleep before all this happened. She said yes, now that she thought about it, he'd had a tendency to cry out at night sometimes.

Then I asked Abraham what had happened while he built the altar. After all, this was a strong kid here. He could easily have run away, and there's no possibility that his old father could have caught him. Did Isaac try to run? Did he struggle when he realized he was to be bound? Protest at being laid on the altar? Abraham said no.

Sarah was about to launch into another tirade when I held up my hand. "Hold on. Let me ask each of you something. When you were Isaac's age, if this had happened to you, would you have run?" They each nodded their heads, yes. "What makes your son unable to stand up for himself? What makes him unable to run away when he's in danger?"

A whole conversation started about Isaac's helplessness, a trait they'd noticed since he was a little boy. I inquired along these lines for a few minutes, and they said that whenever Isaac faced a problem, he would cry or shut down until someone rescued him. The child never learned to stand up for himself. He never had to. "How he acted on the mountain, then, it's just what you would have expected? How he always acts when there's a problem, like someone else will solve it for him?" I asked.

They shrugged. "Yes, pretty much," Sarah said.

Sitting there listening, it dawned on me that Isaac had kept their marriage together for a long time. Well, not exactly Isaac himself—but the talking about Isaac, the worrying over Isaac, the focus on Isaac—that's what had held them together. And they have been sacrificing Isaac for his entire life, keeping him from becoming his own person as they fuss over his every move. If only they would quit treating Isaac as though he were so fragile, he might come out of this a bit stronger.

We talked about Isaac's moaning as his way of asking to be allowed to separate from his parents, to grow himself up. Their three-peas-in-a-pod comfortable togetherness must come to an end soon. After all, they do need to get him out of their tent, if he is to reproduce and this family is to continue.

Your doing-what-she-can diarist,

Emma

Entry 3.7

Seekers' Council—Emma, presenter

Introduction

Today I am reporting on the family of Abraham and the recent event of the almost-sacrifice of Isaac. I am looking for some different perspectives than my own and am glad for the chance to talk with you all. Families are always changing, of course, but this small family unit has seen some big shifts.

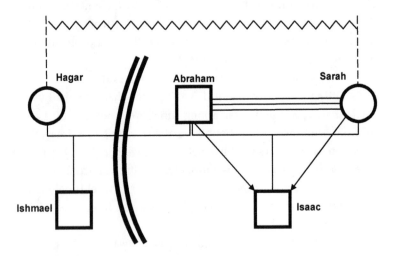

Figure 3. Isaac's family of origin. The chart includes several relationship processes, including the tension (jagged line) between Sarah and Hagar, the intensity of the closeness between Abraham and Sarah (three lines connecting them), the focus of Abraham and Sarah on Isaac (downward arrows), and the cutoff of Sarah and Abraham from Hagar and Ishmael (two-arc lines).

Concerns and questions

Was the almost-sacrifice a predictable event? Given how the processes unfolded in the family over time, it seems to me that each one contributed to the intensity of the Abraham-Sarah-Isaac triangle.

I'm also seeing how Abraham's relationship with his father has impacted his son, Isaac. It's been passed down now through at least three generations—from Abraham's dad to Abraham to his son. How can Isaac, or Abraham, or any person, for that matter, address the problem? My goodness, each generation gets stuck in patterns that existed before they were born!

Council comments by topic

1. Stuck in old patterns

As I see it, what is passed down to the next generation are the patterns of each person's childhood and, most importantly, that first triangle of a child and parents. The patterns of the triangle where one began as a small, totally dependent human being remain somehow within a person, guiding how the person sees the world. They seem to find their way into the rest of life, until a person goes back and works on being different in the first, or original, triangle.

Take Isaac. Look at the original triangle drawn in his family chart. It suggests a person accustomed to being focused on. It suggests little choice about how to respond to either parent—with his thoughts or his emotions or both, according to how he wants to represent himself—instead, his options are limited to his parent's expectations, to which he is exquisitely sensitive. He has little freedom and fewer options than many. He is more stuck. It's all relative, though. My guess is that, for each of us, the centerpiece of growing up—the emotional separation between oneself and one's parents—is never completed.

It's a short jump to seeing that the parents had their own triangles with their parents. The more one can understand what happened in previous generations, the better chance one has of seeing people for who they are. I am not talking here about working out every argument from the past. No. I am talking about separating oneself out as a full adult in the present and getting to know one's family members as real people too.

How does Abraham work on his relationship with his father, who has already died? How does he get to know him as a full person, and not as the parental figure he remembers? One way is to talk with people who knew one's parents in another time or place or in some other setting. If a person can get a more realistic view of their parents, it helps them get out from under the stuff of childhood.

2. Couples

What old patterns from her original triangle has Sarah placed on Abraham? Abraham on Sarah? How does any couple start to see that the problem is not in the other but back in the family? And then, how can they take it back, work on it there, rather than continuing the tension in their relationship with each other?

3. Blaming

I was struck by the way Abraham and Sarah continued blaming each other. How much of the blaming is stuff from the past showing up in the marriage? How can a family get out of the blaming business? How can a family increase its ability to see the larger picture of the family's challenges? When is laughter a help? A hindrance?

4. Underperformance

Isaac has a load of focused attention on him. What has been the impact on him, as you see it? How can he climb out from under all that attention?

5. Adult-adult relationships

With the latest difficulty of his almost-sacrifice behind him, it is time to reflect on how Isaac's childhood is going to shape him in the future. How will he see all this, looking back? How can he start down the path of developing an adult-adult relationship with his father? How can he see his parents and what they were up against so clearly that any bitterness towards them doesn't make sense?

4

The Next Generation

Entry 4.1

Closure

Gen 23:1–2

Dear Diary,

Sarah died last night. May she rest in peace. She was one of a kind. I think about how much I learned from her and wish I had thought to say thank you.

This morning I felt a need to talk with Micah. I found him resting at home, no surprise, for he has lost a lot of energy lately. This morning we talked about Sarah until, at some point, Micah brought up his own dying. As he saw it, he came on this journey out of loyalty to his cousin Sarah, knowing that the family needed him here. With her death, he said, his work was done.

I had known that he might want to talk about something like this. And I know that the day is coming when he will no longer be with us. Talking about it, though, is another matter! At first, I had trouble speaking at all. But he was so calm that eventually I settled in.

We covered some things about the Seekers and how the work would carry on without him. Then, he wanted to know what *I* wanted to talk about. How thoughtful that was of him, vintage Micah. He knew, better than me, that our chats would be coming to an end soon. Not everyone knows themselves so well that they can choose the hour of their death. Well, Micah could.

Does everyone have those *I-wish-I'd-asked-about-that* moments when thinking back on the important people in their lives? When I look back, I see how I avoided real conversations about things that mattered, chatting endlessly about things that did not. And Micah saw that it might happen again this morning. I'm grateful to him for so much.

I took a deep breath and thought for a minute. Then, I asked him whether his thinking had changed about the LORD of Abraham. He said that he was still wondering about the LORD. That he was sure that *if* the LORD existed, that the LORD had purposefully created us within families. Without families, none of us would survive in this world. We are stronger, more resilient in hard times, because we have each other. More than that, though, it is within families that we learn how to relate to others, and in relationships that we become individuals.

Then he talked about being individuals and being together in groups—something about all creation working that way. My attention was starting to drift (he can go on a bit) when he said that sometimes he could sense the presence of family members who had died before him. That they are not exactly watching over him but paying attention somehow. That their presence seems almost palpable at times, as though his ancestors are noticing what he is doing with his life. Noticing and giving him tips, sometimes, along the way! He thought he would be there for me, somehow, after he died. He wondered if I would sense his presence when I write in this journal.

I managed to say that I hoped so. He said that it was clear that his life here was ending and that he was ready to go. His mind was full of wondering what, if anything, might come next. He told me not to let anyone or anything keep me from doing the things I wanted to do with my life—and to have a little fun with it along the way. If I live to be 125, I will not forget this day.

Now I'm thinking about my own death. What am I going to do when I go—I mean, who will continue my work after me?

Perhaps a family member. Not my own children, probably, but someone akin to me, either by blood or by how they think. I'm going to start putting some energy into finding the right person or people and teaching them, as Micah did with me.

Because what we are doing matters. One person's efforts towards becoming more mature makes a difference. It doesn't seem like much at first, but eventually, everyone grows up a little. It's contagious. It's easy to see branches of the family where the maturity is spreading versus branches where the *im*maturity is spreading. I am grateful for Micah and for what I've come to understand.

Your thankful diarist,

Emma

Entry 4.2
The newlyweds
Gen 24:3–6, 17–21, 55–67

Dear Diary,

Today I sat down with Isaac and Rebekah. Who is Rebekah? Oh, let me tell you. Rebekah is Isaac's new wife and *everyone* is talking about it. What they don't know, of course, is what has gone into Isaac's growing up, which had to happen before any of this was possible. Not to take the credit myself—Isaac has worked on getting to know his father and what Abraham had been up against in his own life.

Isaac has a long way to go, though, and he's not helped by the way the marriage arrangement was handled. When Sarah died, Abraham decided to find a wife for Isaac, sending his favorite servant, Eliezer, back to his old homeland to look there. Abraham gave Eliezer specific instructions on the selection of the wife, without consulting Isaac on what *he* wanted and setting Isaac back into his position of the family underachiever. And then Eliezer spotted Rebekah, single-handedly watering all the camels, clearly their family's overachiever. It was the perfect fit—or trap—depending on how one sees it.

Everyone is saying that Rebekah is perfect for him. And she is a capable woman who knows her own mind. She decided to come back immediately to meet her future husband, rather than stay behind with her family as they were urging her to do. She's much younger than Isaac and physically strong too. Have you ever tried watering camels?

You see, here's the question. Can both partners in a marriage be strong? Or maybe that's not the right question. Maybe it's *how* can both partners be strong? What does that look like? Is it possible? For if Rebekah keeps doing everything for him, Isaac will have less self. And if Rebekah keeps taking on the responsibility for others and ignoring her responsibilities for herself, she will have less self also. I remember something Micah used to say: For some couples, it takes two people to make one adult.

It seems clear from what Rebekah said that she grew up doing more than her fair share of the work. Isaac, of course, was the opposite, pampered to an extreme. Today, though, neither of them could see any problem with the arrangement! The honeymoon is not over, I guess. I wonder what else they would like to do with their lives, besides continuing the patterns of their childhoods. Someday, I will ask them. For now, it *is* interesting to see newlyweds. Here is this new relationship—what will they do with it?

Your curious diarist,

Emma

Entry 4.3
Grief

Gen 17:10, 18–25; 25:7–10

Dear Diary,

Abraham has died. May he rest in peace. Ishmael and Isaac went together to bury him in the cave of Machpelah, alongside Sarah, and today, the two half-brothers stopped by to see me.

"I remember the difference you made to my father over his life, and the difference it made for me," Ishmael said. "I know you looked out for my mother and me also. I am grateful."

"I have seen your kindness in my mother's old age, and my father's, too," added Isaac. "And I have heard my parents talk many times about you and the new perspectives you have brought to our family over the years."

"My life," I said, "would have been much poorer without Abraham, Sarah, and Hagar. Let's talk about Abraham today, though. Tell me, what stands out to you about him as a father?"

"He was younger when I was little," said Ishmael. "I remember him as an active guy, sometimes taking me with him when he would go out to the fields to see about the sheep." Then Ishmael laughed. "What I remember the most is the day I was circumcised. Not just the circumcision, although that did make an impression! The conversation we had later that day too. He told me that he had talked to the LORD about me, and that the LORD had said he would bless me and give me twelve sons, princes. And it has happened, just as he said."

"He was older when I was a little guy," said Isaac. "He was not away with the flocks as much. He was around, and that made us close over many years. I am going to miss him, every day."

"He would be pleased that you came together to bury him," I said. When they left, I took some time to think about their visit. Abraham, Hagar, and Sarah, all three, did the best they could with their lives. That their sons would come and see me is a credit to them all.

I am reminded again of the passage of time and the need to find replacements for myself. I've decided to talk with my grandson, Zach, about his interest in becoming a Seeker. He is young, as I was, when Micah asked me. I had a lot to learn, and yet, there is something to be said for starting in one's youth.

Your peaceful diarist,

Emma

Entry 4.4
A new wrinkle
Gen 25:24–28

Dear Diary,

Rebekah has had twin boys: Esau, born first, and Jacob, who came out clutching Esau's heel. They are not identical twins. Esau was born all red and hairy and I can't think of who he looks like. Could it be that Esau reminds Rebekah of someone from her childhood, someone she did not get along with? Because Rebekah already seems to prefer the younger boy, Jacob. I need to remember to ask her, the next time I see her and Isaac.

Today I tried to talk with them about the triangles with their children, such an interesting wrinkle to it when there are twins! Even though I was genuinely curious, I did not have a lot of luck with Rebekah and Isaac. When I sensed their lack of interest, I'm afraid I went from listening mode to teaching mode, and that *never* works.

To be honest, there was one more thing going on. Once I saw that the pattern of focus on the children might repeat itself with the boys, I started worrying about it. Then I started explaining instead of exploring.

I know that when couples get more interested in their children than in each other, more focused on their kids than their own lives, it does not go well for anyone, the kids or the adults. Isaac and Rebekah aren't buying it, though. To be fair, lots of parents fail to see the dangers of focusing on their kids, it comes so naturally when the children are little. I wonder if either of them will catch on to the trap they're falling into. And what to say so that they can see it. And how to keep my own worries out of the way.

Your perplexed diarist,

Emma

Entry 4.5

The stew thickens

Gen 25:29–26:1

Dear Diary,

Isaac came by himself today and wanted to talk about how the boys are arguing all the time. Apparently, the latest quarrel, over a bowl of lentil stew, for heaven's sake, ended with Esau trading his rights as the elder son in exchange for something to eat. Jacob couldn't actually take his birthright, of course, without Isaac's consent. Still, Isaac was acting helpless about his sons not getting along, and not seeing anything he could do about it.

When I noticed myself getting annoyed with Isaac, I thought, What am I reacting to? How can I get more detached? What is Isaac's view? Usually, he's on Esau's side. Would he be now?

I asked him how he understood the situation—if he thought Esau didn't want the inheritance. Or was Esau just reckless?

"No, he's not a reckless child," he said. "He's more interested in hunting than in his fortune, that's all. I can't say that I blame him for that. Being the firstborn is a lot of work and a lot of responsibility."

I think that's the most open Isaac's ever been with me. It gave me a new awareness of the burden on his shoulders as the heir of Abraham's fortune. And it's interesting, Isaac's describing Esau as someone who knows what he wants and goes for it, regardless of what others think or want him to do. I don't think I would have picked up on that.

Esau's still young, of course, and brothers can fight over anything when they're hungry. Still, I wonder, if a family expects a child to perform a certain function and the child isn't interested in doing it, then what? What does the family do? Would it be a marker of maturity in the child or not?

Not that there's a lot of maturity these days. It looks like another famine is coming, and everyone's worried. I remember the last one, when Abraham was alive. Instead of Egypt, it looks like we're heading to Gerar this time. I guess we will make it through. Maybe even prosper, it's supposed to be lovely there.

Yours for maturity,

Emma

Entry 4.6
Off track
Gen 26:34–35

Dear Diary,

The famine is behind us, and life is somewhat easier now. Some things have stayed the same—like Rebekah, who came in this morning to see me. Some things have changed—like Isaac, who is almost blind. His overall health is beginning to fail too. That's not what Rebekah came about, though. She came to complain about Esau's wives—two Hittite women. She was bitter about them and how Esau never comes to see her anymore.

I asked her whether she and Esau hadn't already had a somewhat distant relationship. He's always been his dad's favorite, after all, while she has always doted on Jacob.

"So? I'm still his mother. He and his wives owe me that respect," she said. She was not interested in seeing anything any differently.

I guess I was too direct. I could have asked her *how* she and Esau had gotten so distant, or when the distancing first started. It's easy to get this wrong, Diary, easy to get off track. She moved on quickly, though, telling me in some detail how terrible these new wives were. After she talked about it more, she seemed to feel better, at least for the moment. I, on the other hand, am still put out with myself. I've absorbed her anxiety, and she has no new perspective. It was a wasted opportunity.

Your getting-nowhere diarist,
Emma

Entry 4.7
Baffled
Gen 27:1–29

Dear Diary,

Rebekah came in today and said that she had managed, with Jacob's cooperation, to trick Isaac into giving Jacob the blessing of the firstborn. The inheritance blessing, by the way, is thought to convey power as it is given, so there's no taking it back. Once it's done, it's done.

How she managed it is another story. I have seen some crazy things in my work, but this one is truly unbelievable. Remember me telling you about Esau being hairy? And Isaac being blind? Well, Rebekah had Jacob go in to see Isaac, wearing Esau's clothes and *sheepskin on his arms.* When Jacob asked for the blessing, Isaac noticed that the voice sounded like Jacob's rather than Esau's, so he asked to feel his arms. The goofy sheepskin trick convinced him that the son before him was Esau.

Isaac is upset, of course, and I'm not sure whether he knows that Rebekah had thought of the trick. What made him go ahead when he noticed that the voice sounded different? What kept him from waiting until he was sure who he was talking to? Was Isaac destined to end his life this way—weak and helpless to the end? Will Jacob and Esau make it as adults, or will this side of the family collapse?

The questions were floating around in the back of my mind, but I had to focus. I was floored by Rebekah's story. Baffled. Bewildered. I was trying to keep calm, listen to her thinking, and be a resource to her, without siding with either her or Isaac. When I am with one person in a twosome, I try, in my imagination, to picture the other person there, and to stay on the outside of the triangle.

Back to the situation at hand. All of this would have been avoided if Isaac could have stepped up for once. Everyone wants to blame Jacob for what happened, but I don't see it that way either. Jacob and Esau are the children in this situation. And their parents never figured out how to be reasonable parents to their kids, which goes back to the patterns in the families they grew up in. One would have to go back at least three generations, to Abraham's family patterns, to begin to understand what's happening now.

Yours for getting past blame,

Emma

Entry 4.8
Seekers' Council—Emma, presenter
Gen 27:41–46

Introduction

I have worked with this family for many years, but I am still learning from them all the time. Several recent events have increased tension in the family. Esau married two local Hittite women. Isaac's health has declined, and he now suffers from blindness. Isaac blessed Jacob instead of Esau.

Between the continued hostility between Rebekah and Esau's Hittite wives, Isaac's frustration over losing the chance to bless his favorite son, and the increasing conflict between Esau and Jacob, tension within the family is growing. Rebekah, afraid that Esau will act on his threat to kill Jacob, has asked Isaac to send Jacob away, telling Esau that she wants Jacob to find a wife from among her people, rather than a local girl.

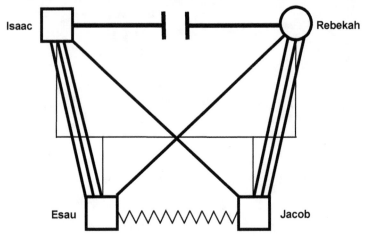

Figure 4. *Jacob's family of origin.* The chart shows Isaac, Rebekah, and their twin sons, indicating the distance between Isaac and Rebekah (a gap in their connecting line), the tension between Esau and Jacob (the jagged line), and the sometimes-intense closeness between Isaac and Esau, and between Rebekah and Jacob (the triple lines).

Concerns and questions

Today I have brought a chart of the triangles between Isaac, Rebekah, and their two sons. As I see it, in the four triangles:

(1) Rebekah is on the outside of the triangle with her husband and Esau.

(2) Isaac is on the outside of the triangle with his wife and Jacob.

(3) Esau is on the outside of the triangle with his mother and brother.

(4) Jacob is on the outside of the triangle with his father and brother.

My interest is in getting clear about the patterns among Isaac, Rebekah, Esau, and Jacob. The patterns didn't begin with Isaac and Rebekah—much of what I'm seeing was going on back in their parents' homes. Still, today I want to focus on these four people and the triangles among them.

Council comments by topic

1. Tension management

Triangles are a useful way of illustrating how families manage stress. Couples can distance, or fight, or focus on a child, or either spouse can be ill. Regardless, though, of what is happening to absorb the tension, it flows through the triangles.

Is it possible to see how stress is handled in this family by looking at how the triangles work? With Jacob away, how will Rebekah, Isaac, and Esau manage the family tension, with one triangle where there used to be four?

2. Triangles in families

Some people seem to have a natural feel for triangles, while others seem to be less aware of how each relationship impacts other relationships. Whether one sees them or not, though, triangles are always present. There is no getting out of them—the question is how well are they working? How flexible would you see the triangles in this family? Can the individuals move around, from the inside to the outside position, or do they remain in fixed places?

3. Death, inheritance, and triangles

Fights about an inheritance usually have something to do with long-standing triangles between children and their parents. It's less about the content of whatever they are fighting over, and more an endless rehash of old patterns. To what extent is the tension between Esau and Jacob a continuation of the triangles each of them had with their parents? When parents die, what happens to the triangles with their children?

4. Triangles with parents

The original triangle—a person with his or her parents—invites a look up the generations. How would you describe Isaac's triangle with his parents? In what ways did that original triangle replay itself with his wife and children?

5. Distancing

To me, the distance between Isaac and Rebekah is the most interesting aspect of the triangles with their twin sons. To what extent did the strong alliance of each parent with one of the children begin with an already-established distance between the parents? Or did the parents begin to distance themselves from one another after they had children? At this point, how do the children get beyond their closeness with a parent? How can Jacob and Esau become selves, when so much of their life has been spent in an intense togetherness with one of their parents?

6. Triangles over generations

I like to look at the triangles in several generations and see what's showing up. From generation to generation, how much of the tension between the children goes back to the triangles with their parents? What are the interlocking triangles, both within a generation and between generations?

5

A Family Split

Entry 5.1
A tough conversation
Gen 28:6–22

Dear Diary,

Rebekah came in to see me today with news of Jacob, who is on his way to her brother Laban's home. It's quite a journey, but Jacob has somehow managed to send a message back to her. It's an amazing story. On his first night out, all alone in the middle of nowhere, Jacob had a fabulous dream—angels climbing a ladder to and from heaven, the voice of the LORD—an extraordinary night.

The next morning, Jacob made a vow about his own life. In it, he talked about the LORD being with him on his journey and about coming back to his father's house in peace, two things that tell me a lot about what matters to him. More than that, though, Jacob's capacity to be clear about his own life interests me. A dream like that might have been overwhelming. He responded to it, though, saying where he stood. It may be a stretch, but I am seeing some parallels to Abraham. Abraham saw that blind obedience was not what the LORD wanted—he talked with the LORD, figuring out his next steps alongside of the LORD. The LORD, it seems, is not interested in puppets.

I asked Rebekah what *she* wanted to do next, at home without her favorite son. What was she going to have energy for now? It was a tough conversation. I had never recognized how lonely she was, living so far from her own kin. The closeness between her and Jacob was how she had survived here. And he's gone. She hopes, of course, that he will be back soon, with a new wife and maybe a grandson for her, and she chatted about that possibility for a while.

All of that, of course, was a way of ducking the question about what she might have energy for now, instead of continuing to live through Jacob, to whom she is joined, regardless of where he is. When we finally got back to the question of what might engage her now, she had no answer at all.

So, I asked what she thought about getting to know Esau better. She laughed at first, after all, she said, she is his mother! Then we talked about getting to know one's children as real people, rather than the childish side one tends to remember from the past. After some reflection, she said that it might be interesting. That there might be more to him than she knew.

She mentioned that after Esau heard Jacob tell Isaac not to marry a Canaanite but to go back to the family homeland to find his wife, Esau decided that he would find another wife, someone from his own people. Rebekah laughed. "I'd been telling him that for years! But when his father said it, he listened."

Well, good for Isaac, in that moment at least, taking a stand. Esau's new wife—one of Ishmael's daughters—might be a needed breath of fresh air for the family. I hope so. It has been a difficult time for all of us.

Your tired diarist,
Emma

Entry 5.2
Next steps
Gen 29:1–21

Dear Diary,

A lot is happening here. Jacob made it to his Uncle Laban's home in Haran. When Isaac and Rebekah heard that he had safely arrived, they started organizing a caravan to take some supplies to them. And I'm hoping to get my grandson Zach on the caravan.

Why Zach? Oh, I might not have told you. Zach has started the work of becoming a Seeker, attending the Council meetings too. He says he's still unsure of whether it's a good fit for him. Who knows?

Over the long run, maybe he'll find the work of the Seekers to be compelling stuff, or maybe not. He is his own person, that's for certain, and this trip will be a good chance for him to think about what he wants to do with his life. If he likes it in Haran, he may stay a while. He's young and unmarried, and it will be an adventure for him at any rate.

My energy flags these days, dear Diary. It is not that I don't think of things I'd like to write about, but lately, I've found I need to save my energy to talk about my thoughts with others, as Uncle Micah did with me. May he rest in peace. I wonder what he would say about Jacob's dream about a ladder? About the LORD not wanting puppets? *Of course not.* I can almost hear him.

Your contented diarist,

Emma

Entry 5.3

Family tricksters

Gen 29:16–30

Dear Diary,

My grandson Zach is back, with news of Jacob, who has married—twice. Laban, Rebekah's brother, had promised his daughter Rachel to Jacob in exchange for seven years of work. After the seven years was completed, Laban tricked him into marrying Leah, the older daughter, instead of Rachel, the younger and, I hear, the family beauty. It was the old veil-over-the-bride trick, and it reminds me of how Jacob had tricked his own father with the sheepskin-over-the-arm ruse. I laugh every time I think of it. Laban's (and Rebekah's) father Bethuel was the youngest of eight boys, and don't you know that Laban had a lifetime of pranks played on him, by his father and all those uncles. Well, he used it well in tricking Jacob, who now has both wives but has agreed to work seven more years in exchange.

There is more news, though. Zach is going back to become Jacob's chief assistant. He's found a wife there too—just one, thank goodness. And he's planning to work as a Seeker there.

As I see it, Jacob and his family need a Seeker with them, as Jacob becomes the family leader. It's still a long way off—years before he can think about coming back. Still, I can see it coming. I remember something Rebekah said when he and his twin Esau was born, that the LORD had told her that *the younger will serve the older.* I don't always believe everything people tell me that the LORD said to them, but her prediction was spot on. Esau is a nice guy. Jacob, I think, is the one who will move this family forward.

And my grandson Zach is going to be working with Jacob. How do I equip Zach? He will be without any other Seeker to work with him, and that will be hard. I've decided to give him this journal as my going-away gift. I will miss you, Diary, and miss looking back at my life through you. Maybe the journal—all that I've written—will be a help to Zach, especially my notes from what Micah said, and the Council discussions too.

It was important to Micah that his work—the Seekers' work—of understanding ourselves, of exploring how families work, and of sharing what we've learned, continue. I should have done more to teach the younger ones. Well, perhaps Zach will learn the practice of journaling, and that may help him more than anything. I know that it helped me.

I do think my grandson and Jacob and his family will be back, someday. I'll be long gone by then, I'm sure. Thank you, Diary, for being here for me all these years. Be with my grandson, Zach. And Micah, if you are listening, please watch out for him too.

Your ever-grateful diarist,

Emma

Entry 5.4
A new diarist
Gen 29:32–30:13

Dear Diary,

Hello. I'm Zach, and my Grandmother Emma gave me this journal and told me to start writing to you. So here goes. I've made it back to Jacob and clan, and on the way, I've had the chance to read the journal top to bottom. It makes me wish I'd listened more when I had the Seekers around in person. Especially Emma. I mean, she's my grandmother and I have lots of memories of her. Still, I'm thinking, what do I know about her work? She never talked about it. And reading this, I have a lot of questions for her now.

One thing I do know—I am not my grandmother, that's for sure. I lack both her wisdom and her experience. But even with all her experience, I don't think she's faced what I'm up against here. Jacob's family is a peculiar challenge, let's say. When he came to see me yesterday, he brought *all four* of his wives—Leah, Rachel, Rachel's enslaved maid Bilhah, and Leah's enslaved maid Zilpah. Both enslaved maids were given to Jacob as wives. Now, Emma had worked with me some on how to meet with couples, but I don't remember her talking about anything like what I faced. Talk about tension.

I did manage to get each of them to talk to me while the others listened, and it's a good thing Emma had written about that. Not much of a start, but maybe something. They did seem curious about what each other might say, and that's a beginning towards seeing each other's perspectives. Will it help them to manage the ongoing tension between them a bit better? Maybe.

Again though, talk about triangles! Put Jacob, Leah, and Rachel together anywhere. Or, put any three of those wives together and watch what happens. It's interesting for sure. That is the one thing I have promised myself about my life—I am not going to spend it being bored. Well, I may have a lot to learn here, but I'm never bored.

One specific triangle—Rachel, Jacob, and any other wife—is rigid. Rachel is always positioned on the inside with Jacob. The result? All the other wives gang up on Rachel. They hate her for being Jacob's favorite. It's hard for me to watch the way they treat her, with the rest of them popping out babies while she remains childless.

I can hear Emma now, kidding me about how protective I was of my little sister and asking me what is getting stirred up here. We had a big sister, too, now that I think about it. Hmmm. Do I treat Rachel like I did my little sister? That won't do her any good. I will become another person protecting her from life and from having to grow up, and she will stay stuck right where she is now. Old patterns are hard to break—Rachel's and mine.

Anyhow, the triangles are constantly playing out. I mean, Leah named her firstborn *Reuben*, which means, *See, a son!* Now that is just mean spirited. But focusing on Leah keeps me from seeing the bigger picture. Maybe the pattern goes back to their triangles with their parents. What was Leah up against? Was Rachel their father's favorite? Hmmm.

Your new diarist,

Zach

Entry 5.5
The big idea
Gen 30:14–15

Dear Diary,

Today I talked with Rachel and Leah. First, I saw Rachel, and I asked her if she had ever tried mandrakes. Emma used to swear by them for women who were trying to have a baby. I know, Diary, I am in way over my head here. *What would Emma do?* She used to say that too much worrying about getting pregnant can keep it from happening. Well, maybe the mandrakes will calm Rachel's worries down, if nothing else.

I also had a long conversation with Leah. She opened up about her frustration with her father, how he had made fun of her poor eyesight as a child and still teases her sometimes. From what she's said, it is not lighthearted banter, or at least, that's not how she experiences it. I expect there's more to the story, more to explore, and I wonder what shaped her father's life.

I brought up the idea of developing a more adult relationship with him. If she can work on being around him without letting his comments bother her, he may stop them eventually. At first, he may try harder to get the reaction he used to get out of her. But if she can hold firm to herself, staying calm, she will get stronger—becoming more of a self, less likely to care about her father's or anyone else's opinion of her, and more interested in her own assessment of herself. And she may get to know her father as a person with his own challenges in life, rather than someone to be feared and avoided.

That's Micah's biggest idea, as I understand it. It's not being more oneself in some imagined world, it's being more oneself with one's family that really sticks—and it changes a person. Back to Leah, though. Right now, she would rather avoid her father whenever possible. She has a long way to go, and don't we all.

Cheers,

Zach

Entry 5.6
Clarity
Gen 30:22–26

Dear Diary,

Two things have happened. Rachel has had a baby—a son, Joseph. And Jacob's decided that he's ready to go home. Something about this child has made him decide it's time to return. I'm glad, of course. Glad to get back to our people and for my own kids to know them.

Still, there's a lot to be done, first. He and I started planning which flocks he'd like to take back, for one thing. In the middle of our conversation, he stopped and said that he'd been way too caught up in helping Laban with Laban's fortune, and not enough with his own.

He was in a reflective mood. His mind went back to the journey here and that first night he spent away from home. He remembered lying there thinking of all he had left behind and how very alone he was. And then the dream, and then waking up with a certainty that the LORD would be with him. And then, promising that if he ever got back home, the LORD would be his God.

I asked him how he thought about his promise now. And he said he thought it was time for him to make good on his end of the bargain. He had to get home. Now here's the thing I'm seeing. He's getting clear about what he's going to do with the rest of his life.

Many people never get this far. They never really choose who or what they are going to serve or how they are going to live. Choice, clarity, what shall I call it? A person—given the situation he finds himself in—deciding who he's going to be in it. That's what I'm seeing in Jacob.

I wonder what Emma would say about the idea of people deciding who they are going to become. I remember her noticing when someone had thought through her own principles and was living according to them. I think that's happening with Jacob, in that he's getting clear and acting on it. It's not about talking. It's useful to talk, and questions can help a person think. But in the end, it's about the doing. That's what makes a person.

Your getting-clearer diarist,

Zach

Entry 5.7
Responsibilities
Gen 30:27–43

Dear Diary,

Is Jacob acting on all that talk? Well, yes, he is trying to gather enough of a flock to return home. However. While he's succeeding with the flocks, it's not going that great with the family. He and his Uncle Laban don't seem to be connecting much these days. Old family patterns of trickery seem to be popping back up.

I'm only hearing Jacob's side of the story, how he's increasing his wealth through breeding practices involving tree limbs, water troughs, and speckled and striped herds of goats and sheep. He tells me he's being up front with Laban about wanting to go home. Whether that's true or not, or how much deceit is being practiced on either side, I have no idea. What I know for sure is that neither Laban nor his sons are happy with Jacob's growing wealth.

Although he's getting clear about what he wants to do with his life, I'm not sure how Jacob sees his responsibilities to the larger family here. He's a little evasive with me these days, which I notice but ignore. It's a lot for him to balance, and easy to understand his predicament.

Today after we got done talking about the sheep (one can only sympathize with Rebekah, and how much she must have listened to her son chatter back in the day, this guy can talk forever) he got started on his wives. He mentioned how the tension between Rachel and Leah seems to be decreasing now that Rachel's had a child. When I asked him what they were thinking about the idea of moving away, though, he said he hadn't asked them about their views!

So, Diary, I just put my own question out there to him. If one gets clear about what one is going to do but has no interest in the views of others impacted by it, what gets lost? We talked for a long time. Short answer: reality, that's what gets lost. And that's what Micah always thought mattered, so I know I'm on solid ground.

We spent some time talking about how to have a conversation with his wives and how to stay interested in how they see it, instead of trying to convince them to agree with him. I broached the subject of his mother and how Rebekah's consistent siding with him may have interfered with his ability to see his wives as distinct people with potentially different views. For a minute, he saw that, and he saw his contribution to the problem. I wonder what he will do with it.

Cheers,
Zach

Entry 5.8
Solo Council—Zach, presenter
Gen 30:1–24, 31:3–5,14–16, 37:35

Introduction

I find myself wishing for the Seekers' Council and the chance to talk about all I'm observing here. I'm getting scattered—it's been a lot to track. Before we begin the journey home, I want to put it all together, complete with a family chart, a summary of the facts, and my questions and observations as they stand now. [*Editor's note: see next page for family chart.*]

Concerns and questions

In the years Jacob spent in Haran, the family unit changed continually. One challenge has been how to manage myself in times of high intensity. When a family's anxiety is high, how does a person work with the pressure, use it rather than avoid it? When and how is it possible to leverage the tension, opening up chances for facing difficulties and solving problems? Another challenge has been that, under stress, family members seem to get confused about their responsibilities for self and to others. As an outsider, I can see it happening. What I wonder is how do people start to see it for themselves?

Comments by topic

1. Anxiety and leadership

People want someone to take away their anxiety, anyone who will absorb it for them. Then they are okay for a little while, and then something else prompts more anxiety. While they do need to calm down so that they can reflect on what's bothering them, the anxiety itself is a good thing—giving them energy to do something about whatever problem they are having. How does a Seeker give people back their problems while, at the same time, giving them a place to get calm enough to be thoughtful? Then, how do they learn to do that for themselves?

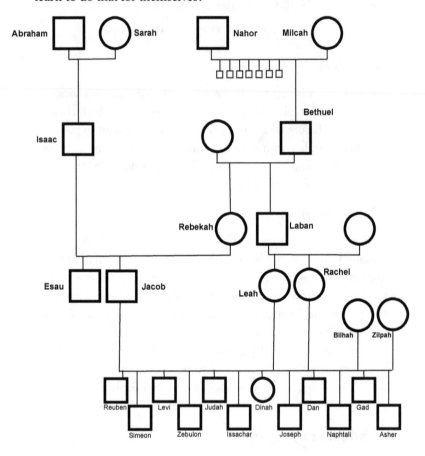

Figure 5. Jacob's family increases. The chart shows the generations above Jacob and the next generation—with Jacob's four wives and children. Jacob married Leah, Laban's oldest daughter, first. She had seven children. He married Rachel next, and she recently had a son, Joseph. He also married Rachel's slave, Bilhah, who had two sons; and Leah's slave, Zilpah, who had two sons. The children were born in the following order: Reuben, Simeon, Levi, Judah, Dan, Naphtali, Gad, Asher, Issachar, Zebulun, Dinah, and Joseph. More daughters were born, but their names were not recorded.

2. Conflict

Jacob's wives and children bicker with one another a lot. No matter what the content, they take the same positions in the triangles, and the tension continues, the same as always. Besides continuing to argue and blame one another, what are their options?

How can they notice the patterns rather than the content of their quarrels? How can a person learn to watch the intensity, refusing to get caught up in it? How could leadership on Jacob's part make a difference?

3. Responsibility

Jacob works hard out in the fields, there is no doubt about that, and he takes his responsibilities seriously. Around his family, though, it's another story. At home, he tells me, he doesn't want to interfere—which means he leaves his wives and children to fight it out, all day, every day. What responsibility does Jacob have to them? How can the same person be so capable in one area and so helpless, almost, in another? How would things change if he stepped up more at home?

4. Triangles

I had suggested to Jacob that he talk with his wives about the decision to return to his home. It was Jacob, though, who thought of having the conversation with Rachel and Leah both together. I am fascinated that they joined in siding with him and against their father. It's as though all they needed was a common enemy to get along with each other. I wonder, how long will the Jacob-Rachel-Leah triangle remain in harmony?

5. Deception

As Jacob prepares to leave, he seems to be avoiding Laban more and more. I am thinking about the time he and his mother tricked his father and wondering if that pattern is showing up again.

To what extent does Jacob's original triangle—close to his mother but distant from his father—continue in his relationships now? Will Jacob come clean with Laban on his plans to leave or not? How does Jacob's relationship with Rachel's and Leah's father, Laban, work? Who is on the outside of the triangle between Jacob, Rachel and Laban? Jacob, Leah, and Laban?

6

Moving On

Entry 6.1
Irreplaceable
Gen 31:26–30, 43–44, 49b–50

Dear Diary,

On the road again! We have left Haran, bringing herds, workers, and families as we travel back to our old home country. I'm glad to be on the way.

We left secretly, but Laban caught up quickly. Even though we had a three-day head start, Laban had neither family nor herds with him, so it was not hard to catch us. The initial greetings were awkward for sure. Laban asked why Jacob had deceived him, saying he would have sent us away with *mirth and songs*. What was more poignant was him asking why he had not been allowed to kiss his children and grandchildren goodbye. It came to me in a flash how much he was going to miss them. When families part, something irreplaceable is lost.

An interesting detail. Laban's clan had their own household gods—a jumble of little objects they prayed to. Laban said they were gone and demanded to have them back. Jacob said that if they'd been taken, he had not known about it, and that anyone found with them would die.

A careful search of the entire camp was made. I noticed Rachel acting a little odd, sneaking over to her camel, mounting it, and, when the time came to search the baggage under her, asking them to skip her bags as she was having her monthly time. I wonder if she took them and, if so, what they mean to her. Does she treasure the trinkets as memories of home and family?

I wonder if leaving her father, who always doted on her, is harder than she is saying. Is she afraid to journey so far from home? How is she going to do without her family nearby? Does her father sense her fear? For when Laban said goodbye, he warned Jacob to be kind to his daughters—that the LORD would be witness to any ill treatment.

Your seeing-more diarist,
Zach

Entry 6.2
A new level
Gen 32:6—33:17

Dear Diary,

Once Laban left, things happened fast. Jacob found out that Esau was on his way—with four hundred men—enough to destroy us for sure, if that had been the intent. Jacob's anxiety went through the roof, and he did everything he could think of to protect both the people and herds on this journey. Afterwards, he was left alone.

That night, I slipped back up the mountain where I knew I would find him. He was wide awake, of course. We talked about the past and what it was like for him to have a twin brother. He talked about the arguments they used to have, how different their interests were, how close he was to his mother, and how close Esau was to Isaac. He wondered about Esau's life and how it had gone for him. I asked Jacob how he had changed, what was important to him now. How could he and his brother get to know each other as adults? He got quiet, and I left.

The story he told later is that a mysterious figure came, and they wrestled all night long. Maybe. I've heard a lot of people recount their dreams, and sometimes they seem so real. Whatever, dream or reality, the result was the same. Somehow, the pressure of the moment crystallized his thinking. In the morning, he was ready to face his brother, to be the person he had become, no deceit, no tricks, only himself.

How did he do it? He told me that he began without an apology or rehashing of past wrongs but with respect now. He restored, to the best of his ability, all that he had taken from his brother, all that the stealing of his brother's blessing had involved. He offered not merely property but also recognized Esau's place, calling his brother "Lord," out of respect for the intention of Isaac's original blessing.

As I would see it, he went with humility, instead of the old family standby of deception. He didn't try to tell Esau what to do or to trick him in any way. He took a stand for himself, and himself

ALL THE FAMILIES OF THE EARTH

only. He found a way out of old, automatic family emotional processes to a more mature, intentional approach.

Esau, too, brought a generous spirit. I wonder what Emma's work with Esau and his mother had to do with the change in him. Together, Esau and Jacob found a way to go forward to best meet the needs of all the offspring of Rebekah and Isaac. They began to relate to each other as individuals, rather than as parts of those old parental triangles, as their mother's or father's favorite.

I do believe, as we head home now, that the family is behaving more maturely. A bit. The use of distancing to manage relationships is still with us—when Esau offered to journey alongside us, Jacob declined. Still, they are talking to one another, and that's a step forward.

Cheers,
Zach

Entry 6.3
Nobody likes change
Gen 34–35; 37:35

Dear Diary,

Never speak too soon. Remember what I said about the family growing up a little? Nope. After we parted ways with Esau, we came to the city of Shechem, where Jacob set up an altar to the LORD. Almost the next thing that happened was that Dinah—a daughter of Jacob and Leah—got entangled with a local boy, and not just any local boy but the son of the prince of the region. The rumor was that he raped her. Dinah herself has been totally silent up until now, so who knows? Still, her brothers, Simeon and Levi, were outraged. I won't tell you all that happened—I'd have to write a whole book. It was a disaster, though, for Dinah and for the people who lived around there. Jacob was furious with Simeon and Levi for stirring up trouble in the area and for destroying local relationships he had worked to build. It was a difficult time.

That's not all, though. At the very end of our trip, right before we got home, Rachel died in childbirth. The baby, Benjamin, is fine. His big brother Joseph, though, is terribly upset. And Jacob is a mess, too, between losing Rachel and then getting home in time to see Isaac, right before *he* died. Oh, and did I mention that Jacob's firstborn son, Reuben, slept with Bilhah, mother of two of Reuben's half-brothers? It's been too much.

Is this what happens anytime one family member starts to act more maturely? Does everyone else go in the opposite direction, trying to get things back the way they were? Not that the way they were was that great, but everyone's comfortable with it, it's what they know. Nobody likes change, even change for the better. Seems like people can smell it when things get out of balance. Is it possible that the family as a whole could sense the difference and was uncomfortable with a new level of maturity? I wonder.

Right now, the biggest challenge is not with the baby, who is well cared for, nor with Jacob, even though he lost both his treasured wife Rachel and his father in short order. The difficulty is with the older boy, Joseph. The poor little guy keeps asking for his mom—you can imagine how she doted on him, after all those childless years. Jacob and everyone else is doing their best to make him happy. No teasing allowed!

I'm reading Emma's notes about how Isaac was protected as a little boy and wondering if that's about to happen again. Every generation thinks they are doing something new and different, but they are following a predictable pattern. One generation produces a certain outcome. Then their kids react, choosing a different path, leading to the opposite outcome. Then with the third generation, it's back to the first.

I'm trying to think of how to be a resource for Jacob. What is in Joseph's best interests, in the long run? How might the experience of losing his mother become part of his capacity to engage life's challenges? I know these are hard questions. I can only ask. Whether Jacob considers them is on him.

Just asking,
Zach

Entry 6.4
A letter from Emma

Dear Diary,

I got so wrapped up in Jacob's family story that I forgot to update you about me. It's great to be home. My wife and kids are happy here, too, and their grandparents are thrilled, of course. Also, it's amazing to be back with the Seekers in person. They've enjoyed hearing what I learned while I was away, and the Council discussions here have helped me to see how to be useful to others in ways I had not understood.

Emma died in the years we were away, and may she rest in peace. She had left me a letter, and I can hear her gentle voice coming through as I read it. Here's some of what she said:

Dear Zach, My days are numbered now. I think of you often and have a thousand and one questions I'd like to ask. I imagine it gets hard for you sometimes, trying to figure things out on your own. I hope the diary is helping. I wonder what it's like, working with Jacob and clan. What I've found in my life is that giving people back their own problems is the best thing one can do. How else do they grow? That's what their problems are for.

Asking questions has helped me too. Even the exercise of thinking of a good question reminds me of my small space in the scheme of things. A good question keeps a person responsible to, not for, the other. A good question respects whatever predicament they are in and signals that it is theirs to manage. Like humility in action, maybe . . .

She went on to talk about our family members and so on, always thinking about everyone, that was Emma. She left a rich legacy, and I hope I can fulfill a piece of it. What a lucky guy I was, to have a grandmother like Emma.

Your grateful diarist,
Zach

Entry 6.5
Dream interpretation
Gen 37:2b–11

Dear Diary,

Joseph is seventeen now. He's a shepherd's helper, assigned to assist his older half-brothers, the sons of the enslaved maids, Bilhah and Zilpah. You won't be surprised to hear that he has a protected status—less helper and more reporter—going back and forth between the fields and his father.

Jacob just had a beautiful, comfortable coat made for Joseph, highlighting his position as the favorite child and making his brothers all the more resentful at the same time. The more Jacob favors him, the more his brothers hate him. For Joseph's part, he's become a tattletale, bringing back a bad report to Jacob whenever he sniffs one out.

Joseph's side of the story? The way he tells it, being next to youngest in a group of twelve brothers is no easy thing. Recently, he told me about a dream he'd had—a thinly disguised imagining of his brothers bowing down to him. Well, given his place at the young end of the sibling pecking order, who wouldn't dream about that? But did he have to go tell them about it? He can't seem to catch on to his own part in the way his brothers are always mad at him. It's so automatic, being on the inside of the eleven triangles with his father and each brother, that he can't see how his position is getting in his way.

Back to the dream though. It suggests something I've been wondering about—is Joseph going to turn out to be the next family leader? I used to think that Jacob's firstborn, Reuben, who shows many of the telltale signs of the oldest child, would turn out to be the family head. But I'm not sure anymore. When Reuben slept with his stepmother, I realized that he lacks a basic part of leadership—self-control. Not to blame him, for I get what he's been up against. As Leah's firstborn, his life has not been easy. How, though, is this family going to survive? Who is going to lead us forward?

Maybe it's going to be Joseph—another firstborn, the first of Rachel's children. When his mother died, and everyone doted on him, he learned how to be charming. People will follow those who captivate them. Still, all he knows is how to get his way. He's got a lot of growing up to do. How can I evoke in him some sense of his responsibility to others? Or interest him in seeing outside the bubble of his own little world?

Cheers,

Zach

Entry 6.6
Family secrets
Gen 37:12–36

Dear Diary,

We've got trouble. It all started with Joseph, who was wearing his fancy coat around constantly. Then, he told everyone about his latest dream: sun, moon, and eleven stars bowing down to him—a story not greeted with a chuckle from anyone, not even his father. Then Jacob sent him to check on his brothers, herding sheep, far from home. They could see him coming on the horizon in his fabulous coat.

The brothers looked at each other and said, *Here comes that dreamer!* They began to plot their revenge, talking about killing him. Reuben diverted them to what might have been a rough but ultimately harmless prank, taking his fancy coat away from him and then throwing him into a pit. I can see how an hour down there might have done Joseph some good—he might have come out of it a bit humbled and stopped lording it over his brothers so much.

However, Reuben left for a bit, thinking that he'd come back later, rescue Joseph, and get him home to their father. But before he could return, the brothers revisited the idea of killing him, or perhaps selling him to slave traders. They debated the ethics of killing versus selling him, as he was, after all, their brother. (For some reason, Diary, this detail bothers me more than anything. I mean, really? Do these guys have no solid principles at all? But back to the story.) In the end, he was pulled out of the pit, sold for twenty pieces of silver, and put on a caravan headed for Egypt.

When Reuben got back, he was completely distraught. They worked out a plan to deceive their father into thinking Joseph had been killed by a wild beast, dipping the fancy coat into the blood of a goat. They (spineless wonders) sent the coat and a message to Jacob, saying that was all they had found of their brother.

Reuben had to talk to someone about what had happened, and so he came to me. We went over his leaving at that critical moment, while Joseph was down in the pit. He said that the chores he left to do weren't anything important. It was more that he felt a need to get away. Once again, distancing was used to manage tension.

Even though I managed to have a reasonable conversation with Reuben, I know that my feelings are stirred up and that I am anything but neutral about what happened. I must, must find a way to get a bigger perspective and calm myself down. Both. I guess that the family is so used to managing difficulties with deceit, they just can't find their way out of it. Jacob was once the son who deceived his dad. And now *he's* both deceived and devastated.

I've tried to talk to Reuben about telling Jacob the truth, but he won't consider it. Emma would have found a way to bring it out into the open by handing the situation back to the family. She could do that somehow, without violating any confidence. Well, I lack her skill, I've always known that, and I've made a serious mistake this time. Somehow, I've gotten myself into the position of participating in a family secret.

What's the best thing for me to do right now? That's really all I've got, right? I can't change anyone else. Never try to talk anyone into anything, that's today's lesson. Focus on what I can do, not on what I want others to do. Of course.

What if *I* go down to Egypt and find Joseph? My family will be okay for a bit, here with everyone else around to help them. And Joseph is going to have to grow up fast, quit acting like a spoiled little brother, or he will get himself killed. I believe I could be a resource. I'm not saying I could free him, nothing like that. I can't free him from slavery or mount an army against the Egyptians. But I can find him, and my presence in the middle of all of this could make a difference. If he had one person to talk to, a thought partner, as Emma used to say, he could make some sense of this mess and figure his own way out.

Wish me luck,
Zach

Entry 6.7
Thought partner
Gen 39:1–20

Dear Diary,

I've found Joseph. Good news—he's alive. Bad news—he's in prison. When he first arrived, he went from slave-for-sale to overseer for an Egyptian captain, but then was accused of raping the captain's wife. Yes, you heard me right. And no, he didn't do it. As I told you, the guy is a charmer. The captain's wife approached *him*, and when he was uncooperative, she had him hauled off to jail with a false charge.

I got busy and found myself a job, assistant to the prison cook. It's steady work and allows me to see Joseph every day. He recognized me right away, even with my Egyptian clothes. We've had a couple of chances to talk. I can tell that his first days as a slave and his recent days in prison have given him plenty of time for self-reflection.

Once Joseph was enslaved, all the years of his father's protection became a handicap. He did not know how to do the simplest things. Like how to care for livestock—simple tasks that any of his brothers could have done without any instruction. Some grim stories of his first days in Egypt came up. Never mind the details, involving a lot of camel dung. Suffice it to say that constant humiliation was the subtext of each day.

He has begun to think about what his half-brothers were up against, with Jacob's focus on him and his full brother, Benjamin, Rachel's other child. I drew some of the triangles on the floor of his cell. It was easy for him to see how the favoritism towards him left his brothers on the outside, time after time.

The next part is going to be a little harder. Can he see his own complicity in what's happened? What was his contribution to the problem? The bottom line—how can he become responsible for himself, rather than spending his life charming others?

Yours in Egypt,
Zach

Entry 6.8
It all adds up
Gen 39:21–23

Dear Diary,

Today I heard the workers in the kitchen talking about the chief jailer, who was looking for someone to help him manage things here in the jail. I mentioned that I knew a prisoner who might be suitable. Someone who would watch everyone carefully. (Nothing like ten unruly older brothers to make one good at that, right?) Of course, I didn't say that part. Anyhow, one of the cooks, trying to get in good with the chief, asked me who it was. And it looks like Joseph may get the job!

I remember reading back in the journal that Emma once wondered—or maybe it was Micah, who wondered about her—and whether she was serving the LORD's purposes. Did the LORD use me for Joseph's sake?

I'm not sure about that. I do think, though, that in life, *everything* gets used. It all adds up. For instance, Joseph really will be good at running things, and that does come from his place in his family. That constant back and forth from his father to his brothers, coordinating all the activities among many shepherds, is going to come in handy here.

Cheers,
Zach

Entry 6.9
Challenging circumstances
Gen 40:1–15

Dear Diary,

Today in the kitchen I overheard some gossip about two prisoners having bad dreams and Joseph's ability to interpret their dreams. I knew instantly that it was time for me to go home. Joseph has become a capable guy, engaging the challenges before him. He's come a long way from the spoiled seventeen-year-old in the fancy coat, always ready to rat out his brothers.

I feel good about it—not just about my leaving here but about my work. I can't do much about the circumstances people find themselves in, but I can ask questions about new ways of managing themselves in them. And leaving them to it—to do their own work, to step up to their own challenges—well, like Emma said, how else does anyone ever learn?

Yours for going home,
Zach

Entry 6.10
Out of the middle
Gen 42:1–8; 50:15–21

Dear Diary,

So much has happened, I don't know where to start. I came home, and we had some good years. I took a break from writing here and focused on training new Seekers—part of my legacy, as I see it. All these years, I've kept quiet about my time in Egypt with Joseph.

Now, though, another famine has come, and along with it, everything has changed. Some of Jacob's sons went down to Egypt to look for food and came back with a story of having met with Pharaoh's governor. This governor had landed the choice slot with his skill at dream interpretation—for he had predicted and planned for the years of plenty and the bad years we're in now. I thought to myself, it's Joseph. But I said nothing.

Well, long story short, a couple of trips back and forth occurred. Jacob first tried to keep Benjamin from going, saying he couldn't lose both of Rachel's sons. Eventually, Benjamin went too—the famine was so bad here, Jacob had no choice but to let him go when the governor demanded it. Once all of Jacob's sons were together in Egypt, the governor, Joseph, let his brothers know his identity.

Now we're all headed to Egypt, to live in an area called Goshen where we can tend our sheep, which Joseph is arranging for us. Without Joseph, I guess we'd have starved to death. It's gotten that bad here.

Just the other night, sitting around the fire—it was Jacob, his sons minus Joseph, and I—something came up about the original tale of finding Joseph's blood-soaked clothes. It was a tense moment, and I decided to use it. I asked Jacob how he thought about that story now. And he looked at me, as calm as I've ever seen him, and said, "I know I was tricked by the blood-stained coat. I've wondered about it for a long time, and I know it now."

And then he looked at his sons and said, "I know you didn't tell me the truth." Just as plain as day, without any anger. And he looked around, waiting. Guess which brother spoke up? Judah. He told the whole story, did not leave out a single terrible detail. And then *everyone* sat there, waiting.

Jacob looked around at his sons and said that he could see the mistakes he'd made in his life. That he had tricked others too. That there was nothing like growing old to give a person the time to recognize their own complicity in things gone wrong. He urged them to talk with Joseph about the past and to ask for his forgiveness.

And then the conversation moved on. Today I'm thinking about how that secret about what had happened to Joseph impacted everyone, and the freedom the family now has to move on. Secrets begin as a place to put the anxiety, but they lock everything down and limit everyone. I wish I could have managed to open up that conversation years ago. Well, I did the best I could with it. It is good to have lived long enough to see the family move on, with more flexibility now.

Your still-learning diarist,
Zach

Entry 6.11
Seekers' Council—Zach, presenter
Gen 49:33, 50:15–21

Introduction

Jacob has died and been buried. May he rest in peace. While Joseph never exactly said that he forgave his brothers for all that happened, he did say that the LORD intended it for good. And life here in Goshen *is* good. We have the Pharaoh's protection through Joseph, pastures for our sheep, and plenty to eat. I am grateful.

Concerns and questions

I am glad to have the chance for a group meeting with you all. So many of my years were spent travelling away from the family, first with Jacob, and then with Joseph. What I've noticed is how stuck a family can get, how they can lose the capacity to find a new direction. My question: How does a family get out of their own historical patterns?

Council comments by topic

1. Patterns

Thanks, Zach, for all you have done for our people over these years. The family chart is fascinating to see. Family patterns indeed. Deceit, protectiveness, and conflict, to name three, are on my mind. What interests me is how automatic the patterns become, and how hard it is for family members to see what they are stuck in. Let's say a person notices a pattern. How do they address it? Is the tendency to distance from it and from the family? What kind of person can stay in the family and retain some choice about following the patterned behavior or not?

2. Secrets

The tendency towards deceit and secretive behavior is a clear pattern. I was interested in the predicament of Zach being caught in the middle of a family secret. How does a Seeker keep things in

93

confidence? When should he? In what way is confidentiality part of stepping to the outside of the triangles?

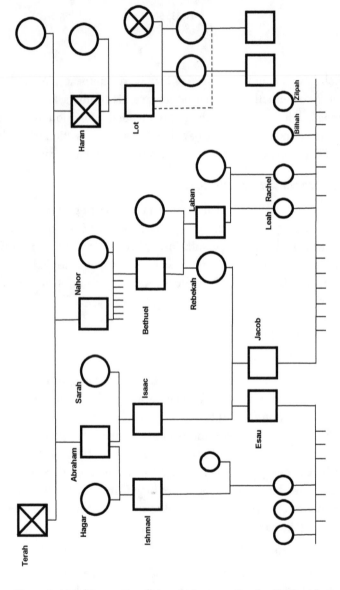

Figure 6. A multigenerational view. **A six-generation family chart from Abraham's father, Terah, to Jacob's and Esau's offspring.**

3. Protectiveness

As I see it, one historical pattern has been protectiveness, which, in my view, breeds immaturity. Jacob's protection of Joseph, Abraham's protection of Isaac, Reuben's protection of Joseph—it's everywhere. Often, protecting others is seen as well meaning, but I see it differently—as doing more to calm down those doing the protecting than in "helping" the protected one.

How can people see the potential damage of protecting others? How can they see their efforts? How does the focused-on child—even as an adult—ever get out from under the "well-meaning" people in charge?

4. Triangles between siblings and across the generations

The conflict between siblings has been noticeable, particularly between Jacob and Esau and between Leah and Rachel. In what ways did the triangles of each person with their parents set these up? And in what ways did the parents' triangles with their parents set up the pattern?

5. Responsibility

I remember your saying that Jacob and Esau managed to find a new way of relating to each other, a more mature way of thinking about their responsibilities for self and to others. How does a family sustain that? What has to happen first?

I can think of several people who got mired down in an astonishingly unrealistic sense of responsibility for (instead of *to*) others, coupled with an abdication of responsibility for self. I think Rebekah was like this, and Reuben, in the next generation. They do in some ways provide a useful function in a family, and they get to enjoy the reliance of others on them. However, as I see it, when responsibility gets located in one person rather than spread over the group, immaturity for the family unit results.

I am wondering how the family can address this pattern of one person doing more than their share and others doing less than theirs. How can they spread it out? Does the move offer any chance to talk about the problem or otherwise work it out?

6. Forgiveness or perspective?

I have been thinking about Jacob encouraging his sons to ask Joseph for forgiveness, and the brothers going before Joseph to beg for forgiveness. Joseph is kind to his brothers, reassuring them that he means them no harm. He never says that he *forgives* them, though.

He had two responses. First, as he saw it, good came from what happened—else the family would have starved to death, probably. Second, he declined the responsibility of judging anyone. "Am I in the place of the LORD?" he asked his brothers. His refusal to let them endow him with godlike capacities was a far cry from the young brother who dreamt of ruling over them. Over the years, it seems that Joseph grew wise.

It seems that blaming others is a waste of time at best. At worst, it fuels bitterness within, while creating less reality-based, more simplistic cause-and-effect explanations. Instead, thinking about one's own contributions to the problem, what one would do differently next time, and what others were up against is a start towards healing. Eventually, one understands so thoroughly that one can say—with all honesty—that *there is nothing to forgive*.

My questions are around relationships. How can conversations about needing forgiveness, or needing someone to ask to be forgiven—with ever-increasing requirements about what should be covered in the request—how can these conversations turn to thinking differently about past mistakes?

How can we follow Joseph's example—without the jail sentence, if possible. Or maybe all of us must do time, jail time or otherwise, to get perspective. How can forgiveness be less about shame and blame and more about growth and understanding? How can a person be less dependent on another's apology and more interested in her own view?

7

Moses and Company

Entry 7.1
Kezi finds the diary
Exod 1:1–9, 15–22

Dear Diary,

Many years have passed since the happier times when Jacob's family settled in Egypt. Zach, the last person to write here, is dead. The Pharaoh who knew Joseph is gone.

It is late at night and I am hiding in a small closet, reading what has been written here by candlelight. Who am I? Oh, of course. I am Keziah, daughter of the midwife Shiphrah. Everyone calls me Kezi.

My mother and another midwife, Puah, are famous among our people. The Egyptians have told them to kill the Hebrew baby boys at birth. But the midwives cover up for the mothers, explaining to the Egyptians that the Hebrew women are so strong that the babies are born before a midwife can get there. It's funny when you think about it—it fits into the way the Egyptians think about us Hebrews. We are dogs, more or less, in their minds, popping out pups unassisted. Still, it is a brave thing, for she and Puah would be killed—slowly and painfully—if the truth were discovered.

My mother wants to train me as a midwife, but I am no good at that. Just the sight of the fluids gushing out of a woman makes me too dizzy to see. Still, my mother is only trying to take care of me. You see, we are an enslaved people now. Midwives are one of the few exceptions to the rule that all must labor, mostly in the fields or making bricks. Soon, I will be made a slave somewhere too.

Life for my people is nothing like when Emma and Zach were alive. I wonder if there *are* any Seekers working these days. There have been no words written here in a long while. I was so lucky to find you, stashed away in my mother's things. Once when I was little, before I could read, I found you tucked away. "Don't touch!" Mother said. She said that long ago, an old man had given her a journal and implored her to hide it. She has no idea that I've found you again and that I'm reading the words of the Seekers now.

Your new diarist,
Kezi

Entry 7.2
Seekers enslaved
Exod 1:8–11

Dear Diary,

I stayed up very late last night, reading what's written here. This morning, I asked my mother if she had ever heard of the Seekers. She shushed me so fast and asked me where I had heard of them. Now, my mother, Diary, you have to understand, there is no use in lying to her. She can smell it or something, she just knows.

So, I told her that I'd read the journal the old man had asked her to stash. At first, she was mad at me. "You would." Then she sighed and said, more calmly, "Of course you would. Yes, I know the Seekers, they are still around. One of them has already noticed you. She said that you might be interested in becoming one of them."

I just stood there for a minute. I don't know what I looked like. I remember how still it was, a quiet around my mother and me, both. "Me?" I asked. "Me," I said. And I remember smiling, just a little.

"Yes. And keep your voice down. Their work is in danger these days. *They* are in danger these days. The Egyptians don't want *thinking* slaves, nor are they interested in enslaved people managing themselves and their feelings, which is what the Seekers are famous for. That's too close to people having a sense of who they are."

"I want to be one of them, Mother. I know it, in myself. That's what I want to do with my life," I said.

"Of course." She sighed again, and for a minute, she looked sad. Then she shook herself and said, "Mothers want only to protect their children. But all of us must be brave in these times and do whatever we can do."

She said that the first problem would be finding labor—forced labor, for my childhood is about to come to an end—still, labor that would keep me positioned, somehow, to do the work of the Seekers. She did not know what it would be. She said that Puah (the other midwife) would know how to connect me to the Seekers, as she is related to one of them somehow. And that I would have to keep quiet, very quiet, about all of this.

Your oh-so-quiet diarist,

Kezi

Entry 7.3
Amazing news
Exod 2:1–9

Dear Diary,

Mother came home today with amazing news. One of the babies she had delivered a few months ago was rescued from a certain death—taken in this morning by Pharoah's daughter.

Jochebed—the baby's mother—had put the child in a basket and placed the basket in the reeds where Princess Bithiah usually bathes. We all know that the princess is kind to us, and I'm guessing that's what Jochebed was thinking. Still, she was too fearful to stay and watch. Not sure if she was afraid of the Egyptians, or if she was afraid to watch what might happen to her baby. Maybe both. What a hard thing.

The baby's big sister Miriam was unafraid and stayed behind, watching from the riverbank. When the princess picked up the basket and cooed at the crying baby, Miriam ran to her, asking if a wet nurse might be needed. Exactly like Miriam—she is a quick thinker.

She and I have been best friends forever, it seems like. She was always the one to climb the highest or run the fastest. Her younger brother Aaron was always running after her. Now their mother is nursing their new baby brother, supposedly *for* the princess, who has named the baby Moses. And get this. While everyone else is enslaved, the princess is *paying* Jochebed for her time!

Miriam stopped by as she was coming back from the palace, carrying Moses with her. The arrangement is that Moses will live at home, with his birth family, until he's weaned, and then he'll live at the palace. In the meantime, Miriam gets to take him back and forth whenever the princess wants to hold him or play with him.

My mother asked Miriam about the palace where the princess, Bithiah, lives. Were there any enslaved Hebrews working there? Did she see any possible openings for us? Would they be interested in us? She said it would be better if we were both working there and could look out for each other. Miriam is going to talk to her mother about the idea.

Yours, I hope, at the palace,
Kezi

Entry 7.4
Hiding the diary
Exod 1:12–14

Dear Diary,

Miriam and I are now working as slaves at the palace. It's not great work—I'm scrubbing floors—but it beats making bricks or working in the fields, which is what most of my people are having to do. And don't worry, you are carefully hidden, wherever I am— if you were discovered, I don't know what would happen to you or me. I will be careful to keep you a secret. And I don't have much chance to read anyhow. I am kept working all the time—sunup to sundown.

The one piece of good news is that I now have a connection to the Seekers at the palace. One of them, Mered, a cousin of the midwife Puah, was a great-great-grandson of Zach. Even though he is a Seeker, and related to Zach, he did not know about you, Diary. He has visited me several times to look at the entries. It's funny. He will read for a while and then walk away, talking to himself.

Mered and several others have continued the work of the Seekers, talking with people in hushed tones, while making bricks or whatever task is required that day. He also has duties at the palace, where he comes to report to the overseers about brickmaking. Occasionally when I see him, he talks with me about the basic ideas, like the need to stop blaming individuals. He says to try to see everyone involved in a situation and get each person's perspective. I am grateful that I get to learn from him.

Mered doesn't hold a grudge against the Egyptians. He says that all of us like to see our own group as better—or at least different—from other groups. The Egyptians calling us lazy, or stupid, or whatever is what all tribes do to each other. He says that wisdom involves something besides clumping a whole group together—instead, seeing each person for who they are.

Well, you can believe I've not gone back and told anybody at home this one! Part of being wise is knowing when to say a thing.

Still, I'm pondering the idea of the Egyptians being people, just like us.

Take Princess Bithiah. I clean all the floors in her part of the palace, so I see her a lot these days—and I see Miriam too—we do some of the big rooms together. Anyhow, Princess Bithiah treats everyone with respect—her own people *and* us. And she requires the people working at the palace to do the same, as much as she can.

Some of the Egyptians are good to me. A few, I would even count as friends, especially Phari, an enslaved Egyptian who works the hand mill in the palace kitchen. She, Miriam, and I giggle all the time, until a guard comes around, when we hush.

Yours at the palace,

Kezi

Entry 7.5
Moses
Exod 2:10

Dear Diary,

I have not dared to write in a long time. Life has gotten much harder on all of us Hebrews. They—the Egyptians, that is—are making my mother work in the fields. I cannot believe it. Even when she's been up all night with a difficult birthing, she must go to work in the morning. But that's not the worst of it.

Yesterday, the princess was gone when the guards caught Miriam playing with Moses instead of working. I was in the corner, scrubbing floors as always. What happened next was awful, let me warn you. They shoved her down, then kicked her around, for good measure, apparently. Moses got between them but he's no match for their strength—he's just a boy. They stopped hurting her though. Probably having to deal with Moses gave them a minute to recognize that if they went too far, the princess would cause trouble for them. They got Miriam up, told her she would be assigned somewhere else, and led her away.

I was left there, afraid to stop scrubbing lest they take me too. Moses was crying and shaking. I got him something to drink. He pulled himself together and watched me work for a while.

"I hate them. I hate what they are doing to our people," he said, in his halting voice. "When I grow up, I will make it stop."

It dawned on me that my life's work was beginning. What to say? For sure, it was not the right moment to talk about respecting the Egyptians. What would be useful to Moses, I wondered.

Then it came to me, something Emma had written here, about saying back to a person what they had said. It gives the person a chance to clarify their own thinking, which is what they need to move forward, *and* it buys me time to sort out any questions I might ask. A simple restating was all I needed to do.

"You are going to make it stop," I said.

"Well, not by myself, that won't work. But our people are strong. We are not so helpless as the Egyptians think."

"Not quite so helpless," I said. And then I realized that Moses was feeling helpless. More than that, though. I saw that he was finding his own way through it, that he was already less overwhelmed. I thought, how does a person manage the feeling of helplessness? Maybe that would have been a better question, or a good next question. By the time I had thought all this through, though, I noticed a different expression on the face of Moses.

He looked at me and it got very still, the quiet enveloping us like a cloud. "I will never forget what happened to Miriam today," he said. "I will grow up and be stronger. I do not know what will happen to me, but I do know that I will never watch my sister get hurt, nor any of my people suffer, without doing what I can to make it stop." He stood up, wiped his tears off his face, and left me there, scrubbing the floors.

I had all day to think about what had happened. I thought about Miriam and hoped that she was all right. Then I thought about Moses, and the back and forth that went on within him, between his thoughts and his feelings. And I thought about how I had made a difference, how good it was that someone was there for Moses. I was all the more amazed that my words had made some sense—had helped him think.

Mered came by after he heard the news and told me he'd check in with the princess to see what could be done for Miriam. When I told him more about the day, he got interested in how Moses had handled himself, both with the guards and after they left. He said those moments when a person gets clear enough to say what *I will or will not do* are big ones, whatever the subject. And that although he never would have guessed it, that Moses may turn out to be a leader, just the leader our people need.

Your new Seeker,
Kezi

Entry 7.6
Tension up
Exod 1:9–10

Dear Diary,

Moses is around less these days. I barely see him at all now that he's taken up Tahtib. What's Tahtib? Well, Diary, it's a sort of Egyptian stick-fighting. He only comes by, his *asa* (stick) in hand, to show me his latest skills—and to check on me, I think. Everyone is a tad tense these days, trying to watch out for each other.

Mered and I were talking about how anxious we all are when he reminded me that the Egyptians are no different—every group is looking out for its own. Just as our families are always looking for a way for the next generation to carry on, so also are Egyptian families. It's our success as a people, that we have grown in numbers, that is making them nervous.

Still, understanding takes one only so far. I'm a bit afraid, all the time, now. Ever since the guards took Miriam, I try to stay close to the princess whenever possible. She does not always know I'm around, but usually, I am within earshot.

And today I heard her and Mered talking. In their voices was a tenderness that I had not heard before. I glanced around the pillar to see Mered touching her cheek, ever so gently. And her looking back at him—oh my goodness, the look in her eyes! You don't suppose?

Wondering,
Kezi

Entry 7.7
A conduit
Exod 2:11–15

Dear Diary,

We have a problem. Moses has done the craziest, dumbest, most unbelievable thing. He has killed an Egyptian. Killed.

He was shaky when he first showed up and told me what had happened. I told him to go splash some water on his face. He came back in a few minutes, a tad calmer. *He* was calmer, that is. I was not. I was trying to think for both of us, and then it dawned on me that I needed to hand him back his problem.

"First things first, what are you going to do next?" I asked.

"Next?"

"Well, what will Pharaoh do to you, when he hears? Who saw it?"

"No one, I think. I looked around first."

"Right." I snorted. I tried to stop myself, but I snorted. "Chances of no one seeing something like that are small, I think." Then I noticed how upset I was. *Not useful!* I thought, and pulled myself together a bit, trying to focus on this new reality. Handing a problem back to someone was harder than I had thought it would be.

"Tell me about what happened," I said, once he had caught his breath and I had calmed myself down enough to think.

He said that it all got started when he saw an Egyptian beating his cousin, Jerry. Back when the children were little, Miriam used to bring Jerry to the palace to play with Moses.

"There was no way I was letting that guy hurt Jerry," he said. "That's all it was, at first, me getting between them to stop the beating. Then I just got so mad. I only hit him one time. I did not have my *asa* with me, but I hit him hard."

He went on and on about how he'd done the right thing, that it was long overdue, and that there was more where that was coming from, and so on. He described all the cruel things that had been done to the Hebrews with a bitter voice. I didn't answer—just sat with him.

Finally, he hung his head and was silent. He said he was sorry—sorry that he had done this thing. That he could still see the look on the Egyptian's face in that split second when he knew he was going to die. He said that Bithiah had taught him that the Egyptians were people, too, that they were not to be treated cruelly, just as the Hebrews should not be.

Then, he talked about the day when Miriam got kicked around and deciding to get strong enough to stand up to people, to stop their cruelty. But he had gone too far. The anger, he said, had taken over.

We talked about the capacity to manage oneself when emotions are running high. I worked hard, Diary, neither to comfort nor to accuse him. I saw in that moment that *life* was teaching him, not me. I was, at best, a conduit for the lesson being offered.

"Look, I'd like to talk more," I said. "I'm afraid, though, that you might have been seen. What's your backup plan?"

"Backup plan?" He thought for a moment. "I could go to Midian. It's not too far, and yet it's remote out there. Not a place where the Egyptians are likely to go."

Today he is gone. Rumors are flying around about what happened, so I'm sure he has realized he's in danger.

Your sleepless diarist,
Kezi

Entry 7.8
Compelling clarity
1 Chr 4:17

Dear Diary,

Things are very quiet around here, with Moses gone, the Pharaoh looking for him, and the princess keeping her thoughts to herself. It is not a peaceful quiet—no, more the opposite—an intense, everything-is-about-to-explode kind of quiet. Today, I heard the princess and Mered talking about Pharaoh's anger, the worsening situation for the Hebrews, their cries for help, and how sad it was for everyone.

Then it got quiet. I guessed that they were embracing, but I dared not look, lest I spoil my cover. And then I heard him ask her to marry him—yes, *marry* him—when the Hebrew people were free. That he would marry when his children would be born as free people, and not into enslaved families. And she said she would wait for him, until the Hebrew people were free. Not a day longer, she said with a laugh.

If I live to be 125, I will never hear a more romantic conversation. More than romantic. It reminds me of what Mered said once, about people getting clear about what they would and would not do. Who knew that clarity could be so compelling?

Your stunned diarist,

Kezi

Entry 7.9
Perspectives
Exod 2:12—8:19

Dear Diary,

Enough time has gone by for the Pharaoh to forget what Moses did and move on to other worries. Moses is back with a Midianite wife, Zipporah, and two sons. Bithiah was thrilled to meet them today, and Moses had lots to tell us about his time away. Zipporah's father, Jethro, is a priest in Midian, of all things! But Moses's most interesting story was what happened while he was shepherding for Jethro. *He saw a bush that was on fire but did not burn up.* He was serious. As he went closer to see it, the LORD spoke to him.

"Who? What LORD?" I asked. And then I remembered. I've read about the LORD here, from what Emma and Zach recorded in the early days of our people. But no one ever talks about the LORD anymore. Until now. Because Moses is putting it out there for everyone to hear, that the LORD of Abraham, Isaac, and Jacob is back, big time.

He's skipping the slightly crazy part about a voice coming from a burning bush, lest people think he's been out in the desert too long. We had quite the conversation about the burning bush, and he concluded that the details of how and where he heard the LORD did not need to be shared. The main point is to deliver the LORD's demand—that Pharaoh let the Hebrew people go so that they may worship the LORD in the desert.

He's saying all this through his older brother, Aaron. While Moses is less than articulate, Aaron is quite a smooth talker. Still, it's a no-go with Pharaoh, who is one stubborn guy. Miriam's guess is that he's used to getting his own way—after all, he has for his entire life. He simply can't imagine that he might not, this time. Moses says that the LORD is making Pharaoh stubborn.

Aaron has a different perspective. He said that Pharaoh is a politician, and he knows that he doesn't have enough Egyptians on his side to let us go. Leave it to the middle child to notice the alliances, right? Aaron said if he tried to let us go now, that the Egyptian people would not go along with it. He said that there would be a power struggle—and that Pharaoh would lose. Then, the Egyptians would round us up and bring us back and make our lives even more a living hell.

Wow. As powerful as Pharaoh is, he still rules at the consent of his people, who like having enslaved people around to do their bidding. Aaron said that Pharaoh will change his mind only when the Egyptian people want to let us go.

Well, that's going to be a while, for sure. Pharaoh and his crew responded to the request of Aaron and Moses with new demands. Now, laborers must go out, gather their own straw, and make the same number of bricks as before, when the straw was provided to them. Which of course is impossible to do, and then the beatings start. Every day. I don't remember the last day I did not hear the whiplashing, the screams, the whimpers.

Not only that. There have been three plagues, so far—water in the Nile turned to blood, frogs, gnats—all horrible, and what terrible smells, here at the palace. People are blaming Moses for it all. It's like they don't have the energy to think—they just want a simple explanation, complete with someone to blame.

Your struggling diarist,
Kezi

Entry 7.10
Seekers' Council—Kezi, presenter
Exod 8:20–32

Introduction

I am grateful for the chance that the latest plague has given us to meet here in Goshen, under the cover of flies inflicting the rest of Egypt.

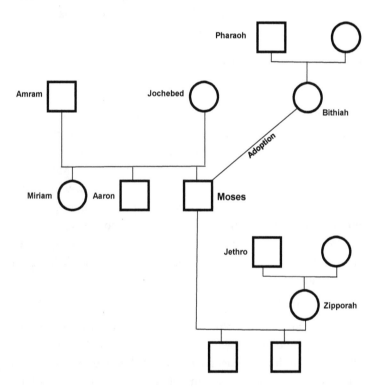

Figure 7. Moses's family. **Moses was born into the family of Amram and his wife, Jochebed, during the time of the Egyptian persecution of the Hebrew people. He was adopted by an Egyptian princess, Bithiah. As a young man, he fled to Midian after killing an Egyptian. He married Zipporah, had two sons, and returned to Egypt.**

Concerns and questions

I'm going to talk about the family of Moses, whom I have known all my life. I know my subject, but at the same time, it may keep me from seeing some things about them.

While I am concerned about the amount of pressure that the family is under now, I am seeing a lot of strengths. Aaron has been not only a good communicator but an important partner for Moses in sorting out the political realities involving Pharaoh. Moses's own experience of growing up in both the Egyptian world and the Hebrew world is a strength in these difficult times. It has been interesting to watch the family work together.

Council comments by topic

1. Anxiety

Kezi, your mother and the other midwives have been brave women, risking their own lives to give our baby boys the chance to live. And now, here is Moses, one of those baby boys, fully grown and working to set his people free. The pressure on Moses and Aaron and the entire family is important to consider. In a time of great tension and adversity, when everyone is under pressure, how do the leaders use the tension, leverage it to the benefit of the group? I wonder, in this situation, how all of us can learn to see some anxiety as a good thing—necessary to face the challenge of getting out of Egypt?

2. Blaming

Some are blaming Moses for everything that's happened, for the beatings and the hunger, as though Moses himself were responsible for it all. It's like they have stopped thinking for themselves and just want someone to blame. I wonder if this has anything to do with our many years of slavery, of not having to—or being allowed to—think for ourselves. Has blaming just become a bad habit? How do we as a people get out of it?

3. Multiple perspectives

Moses has an Egyptian princess as his adopted mother and a foreigner as a wife, so he has a lot of experience with knowing people from different backgrounds. There is strength in that mix. How can he draw on that experience? You have worked with him in the past, as I understand it, to manage his anger towards the Egyptians. How might he be reminded of that work, or revisit it, or expand on it? I believe that energy gets lost when people spend time reviling others instead of trying to understand them. The question, though, is about more than Moses. How do all of us work on seeing what the other is up against?

4. Triangles involving groups

I am interested in the different ways of looking at Pharaoh's so-called stubbornness. Too often we attribute a problem to an individual, when it is more realistic to see whatever is happening as a reflection of a bigger reality. I think Aaron's way of looking at it, as not in Pharaoh himself but a result of his position in the middle of tension between the Egyptians and the Hebrews, makes sense.

Essentially, it's a triangle, and Pharaoh cannot find a way to get to a comfortable outside position. He is stuck with both sides putting pressure on him. Blaming him or anyone gets in the way, in my view. Understanding matters.

5. Reasoning

People are very different in their ability to manage their emotions. Some people let their feelings run everything—even their minds, finding the cleverest ways to explain away what were, essentially, thoughtless choices. Like killing someone.

What would Moses say now about what he learned when he killed the Egyptian? How has that experience changed him? How can a person learn to go back and forth between their thoughts and their emotions, listening to and employing both in their reasoning?

8

Freedom

Dear Diary,

More plagues came, Diary. The Hebrew people were spared the worst, as the plagues skipped over Goshen. But I was stuck at the palace. The thunder and hailstorms, the locusts and the darkness made it too hard to leave. I did make one trip to check on everyone at home—and to be with them too. My parents, old and wise, assured me that they are ready for whatever comes. Their fearlessness spread directly to me. I am ready now too.

Moses kept talking with Pharaoh—through Aaron, of course. But Pharaoh continued to refuse to let us go. One thing you have to say about the guy, he was consistent. If it was Pharaoh's goal to make it harder for the Egyptians to want us to stay, he was on target.

In the meantime, Moses gave instructions for every Hebrew household to prepare a feast—with specifics on selecting and preparing a lamb for the meal. He said to gather in our homes to eat. He even told us what to wear—that we should be dressed ready for travel, right down to having our sandals already on our feet while we ate.

He also said some, well, crazy-sounding stuff, even with all that's happened. He talked about an angel of death. To avoid being visited by said angel, he said to mark the doorposts of our homes with blood from the lamb. Well, the princess and I, sitting in the palace, could not do that part. But we were sitting there eating roasted lamb. Until we began to hear sounds of people crying and screaming in the night.

My friend Phari here at the palace—an enslaved Egyptian—had gone home for the day. She came back, though, shaking all over and saying that her sister's baby was dead. She described an "angel of death" killing the firstborn child in every Egyptian home.

I was trying to ask her to tell me more when she interrupted. "No matter what it is, or was, you must flee. Run before someone finds you, for surely any Hebrew found tonight will be killed." We embraced, but she said, "Quickly now, go."

"Phari, I am so sorry. I do not want to leave you," I said.

"I know. But you must go on your way. And I must go back to my family. They need me now." And she left.

Bithiah had heard us talking. She came in and showed me the way to a secret passage from the palace. "We knew this day was coming," she said. We ran silently, underground, for a long time, it seemed to me. It was dark, and the lantern we were using was not much help. I wondered where we were going and what we would do when we got there. Finally, we started going up, towards a bit of light. But when we got close to the door, Bithiah stopped.

She told me to sit down. There were jugs of water there, and some food, and a change of clothes for her. I thought, how clever, a disguise. But she said, "Not a disguise. Who I am to become. A Hebrew wife."

We had a long wait, to the wee hours of the morning, and plenty of time to talk. She told me that watching Moses grow up and become a leader had helped her to see her whole life differently. She talked about deciding to adopt Moses. "When I saw him, I knew instantly. I could not save all the babies, but this one, I would. I was determined. I took a lot of criticism for it. But now, that decision is giving life back to *me*."

"How is it giving life back to you?" I asked.

"Well, I don't know, exactly. I don't know how this is going to work out. Will it make a real difference, or will the Hebrew people end up back in their chains? We will see, over the next few days. But if it goes wrong, Kezi, and I die, do not mourn for me. I have a peace or maybe a satisfaction that I have done what I could. That's what I mean. Acting on my own principles, that's what has given me life." She stopped, thinking.

"Not only that," she continued. "It's all of us. Take my son, Moses, or you, or your mother, or Miriam, my goodness, she was just a child herself that day, when I found Moses in the basket—many, so many—have stepped up. No matter what happens, I think each of us has done the best they knew how to do." She closed her eyes, and we rested for a while.

When Mered got there, his eyes locked on us. "Find your strength. We'll be fine once we get to Succoth, but we must hurry now." And to make a long story short, we made it. That first night, Mered and Bithiah married in a celebration like none I have ever seen, before or since. Everyone was happy to be alive. And to be free.

Your unenslaved diarist,
Kezi

Entry 8.2
Celebration
Exod 13:17—15:20

Dear Diary,

We followed a pillar of cloud by day and a pillar of fire at night, camping at Etham. Then we moved on, which attracted the Pharaoh's attention, and he led an army to find us and bring us back. We were terrified. All of us—families with old people, parents, children, and all we could carry, on foot—with a professional army, complete with chariots and horses, coming after us.

The usual blaming of Moses had begun again. Then, the cloud we'd been following lifted and moved behind us, blocking our view of the army and their view of us. In front of us was the Red Sea, and it got so windy that the waters started to part. Someone started running towards the opening, and before long we were all following. When we were safe, the waters started coming back, and the Egyptians followed us no more.

Miriam started dancing and pounding on her tambourine, "Sing to the LORD, for he has risen up in triumph." I have never seen Miriam so joyful, so happy, so *playful*. Soon all the women were following her in the dance. Well, almost all the women. I watched and wondered how to understand all that had happened.

Miriam's words were spot on. Not only was it time to be grateful, it was time also to note that we Hebrews did not do this by ourselves. Something beyond us was and is happening. Is it the LORD of Abraham, Isaac, and Jacob? I don't ever remember anyone talking about the LORD, in all my life, until Moses came back from the desert with the burning bush story.

Oh wait. That's not true. There's also what I've read here. I wish, Diary, that you could talk back to me today. I hope everyone who wrote in here—and everyone they wrote about—knows what has happened. Maybe they are here, celebrating with us today. If my eyes were clearer, perhaps I could see them now.

Good night,

Kezi

Entry 8.3
Bitterness
Exod 15:22–25

Dear Diary,

Miriam came to see me today and started right in. "So many family members I thought about last night! It's important to remember them now. They are a part of us getting here." I mumbled something and she kept right on talking. "I keep remembering how I would listen to them—my parents, my grandparents, may they rest in peace—whispering late at night, thinking that the children were asleep and would not hear the awful, horrible details of their lives. And then they'd talk about *someday, when we are free.* Well, that day is here."

I kept quiet, sensing that there might be more. And there was. "But I don't know that they knew how hard this part was going to be. We've walked for three days and finally found water. Then when we run up to it, we find that it is bad water. People can die from drinking water that smells so bitter, so foul. We can't go on much longer like this."

Well, I thought, now what? We are all terribly thirsty, she's right. How can we get some perspective? And get our minds onto something else too? "We are in a bad way," I said. "I wonder what our grandparents would say to us, if they were here. How hard do you think it was for them?"

"Maybe harder than I realized. Maybe hard to know that you are going to die and that your children are still going to be enslaved, no matter what you do. Now that I think about it, I'm remembering stories about *their* great-grandparents, the stories they'd heard from the first to be enslaved. How bitter they were at their change in fortune when the Pharaoh who knew Joseph died!"

"Sounds like bitterness has been in your family for a long time. Do you want to keep it going?" I asked.

She laughed, a rueful laugh. "I'm good at it! How does one find a new way when there is so much to be bitter about?"

We talked some, about the history of our people and how it was back when the Pharaoh knew Joseph and we were held in esteem. And then, the sudden descent into slavery—what must have been initially shock, then horror—and then an everyday anxiousness that settled in. When we walked outside the cave, we heard that Moses had found a piece of wood and (at the LORD's direction) had put it in the water, making the water no longer bitter!

Revived,
Kezi

Entry 8.4
Finding a new way
Exod 16—17:7

Dear Diary,

Miriam came back today. We exchanged a few pleasantries about our new diet—manna and quail in the wilderness—*everyone* is talking about it. Then the conversation shifted to the days when she and I were both working at the palace. We were enslaved, of course, but we were house slaves, and relatively safe.

There was a lot I didn't know about the years after she was thrown out of the palace. Things got very rough for her. She went from her job at the palace, a job where she was a bit protected and which held meaning for her, looking out for her baby brother, to being a field hand. Extra helpings of cruelty were added on because of her former protected status at the palace. It was brutal. She was singled out, handed over to those who enjoy inflicting pain on others, and used as an example to keep everyone afraid.

I listened for quite a while. The bitterness, the frustration, the pain, it was all there. I wondered what would be useful to her now. The helplessness of being enslaved was a thing of the past, or at least it could be, but not if she's still stuck, still bringing it into the present. It was a tad lighthearted, but I wanted to shake her loose a little, so I asked her, "Is the Miriam I know still there? The one with the take-charge attitude?"

Turns out, that's what she's wondering too. She was happy when we were first safely across the Red Sea. The resentment, though, is already taking over again. The lack of food and water these days in our desert life is getting her down, reminding her of days when all the enslaved people went without anything to eat or drink if impossible work quotas went unmet.

Well, Diary, this was a difficult conversation. I had some terrible experiences as an enslaved person, even with my protection at the palace. I've never written about it and never will. But it *was* awful. I wanted so much to join with her, to bond over how bad it was! Somehow, I caught myself and focused.

I said that I'd noticed that people were having all kinds of reactions to the current difficulties. Some were bitter. Some were complaining. Some were helpless, ready to give up already. Some were silent, morose.

"It's like each of us has a built-in way of dealing with challenges or avoiding them altogether. Our years of being enslaved have added a layer of difficulty," I said.

"Yes," she said.

"What would you say is automatic for you, in hard times?" I asked.

"That's easy. Bitterness. Resentment. Helplessness. All three."

"The way I see it, somehow these automatic reactions get set in each of us, at an early age. It's whatever a person has gotten used to doing."

"For sure. From the time I was a little girl, I was the big sister, taking care of Aaron, and then Moses, too, making sure they were safe. It was hard. It was necessary, though. Not only was my mother enslaved, but other family members and neighbors who might have watched over us were enslaved too. All of us children had it rough. I did my best to take care of both my brothers and get the meals and all. Sometimes, it mattered. Like with Moses, he might not even be alive today if I hadn't watched over his basket."

"You were there for Moses and Aaron."

"Yes. Still, Aaron is my parents' favorite, and Moses is Bithiah's favorite. I was nobody's favorite. I'm just the one who takes care of everybody else."

"Just the one who takes care of everybody else," I said, repeating her exact words, not wanting to add to or take away from her own thinking.

Miriam went on. "What I do remember is that it was never enough. No matter how hard I tried, I was always coming up short. Everything I did could always have been better. Of course. I was just a child myself, and nothing I did was ever right. And my brothers always needed something else."

"So you were a little girl, and trying very hard."

She nodded and then covered her face with her hands.

123

"What would you imagine your mother would say, if she were here now?"

"She would say that she counted on me in a way that she didn't count on my brothers. That she loved me too. I know she did. We were *so* close. It's almost like we were the same person. I knew what she would want me to do without even asking," Miriam said. I could see her face relax as she remembered.

"Now that we are free, there is more time to think about our families. Many people knew your mother. She worked in the fields with a lot of people."

"That's true!" she said. "I can ask them how they remember her. There was so much she avoided talking to me about, trying to protect me."

"I have one more thing to ask you. Was it ever an advantage to be nobody's favorite?"

Miriam sat up straight and laughed. "Yes, now that I think about it, sometimes it was great. Nobody bothered me," she said. "I did all the work, but I had more latitude, more freedom, than my little brothers. I wonder," she said, laughing again, "I wonder if they got tired of being fretted over. I should ask them."

I wanted to go back and explore how to redirect herself now into taking charge of her own life rather than continuing the big-sister-responsible-for-others position. But I decided it was time to stop. We were both getting tired. And the last thing she needs is another person to please.

Your satisfied diarist,
Kezi

Entry 8.5
Leadership
Exod 18:1–13

Dear Diary,

Early this morning I had a visit from a natural-born leader. Moses? Nope. Moses is learning, but it is not easy for him. The born leader is Jethro, father-in-law of Moses. He's traveled here with his daughter Zipporah and the boys she's had with Moses. They are good kids, by the way, and it's fun to see them again. Moses had sent them home to live with Jethro for a while. He's brought them back now that the immediate danger from Pharaoh's army is over.

Jethro got right down to business. He's been here only a short while, but he had many questions. "What is happening here? It looks like Moses works from dawn to dusk. And the people just wait for him to tell them what to do. What a bunch of babies! Do your people not know how to decide anything without him?"

"Well, that's a good question," I said. I had to stop and think for a minute. "What do you think is going on? Do you suppose we've forgotten how to decide things, after so many years of slavery? That we are just used to being told what to do?"

"I'm not sure. It's the work of the LORD that you have gotten this far, that much I know. But you will never make it out of the desert as a people if you all don't face the new challenges of surviving in the wilderness," he said.

We talked about the problem for quite a while, with Jethro describing Moses sitting there listening to every problem that was coming up during the day and trying to figure out what to do about each one. It would have been hilarious if it were not so true. He said that the indecisiveness and lack of responsibility people were showing would not serve us well. Resourceful people, he said, know how to manage themselves.

"Could you share these ideas with Moses?" I asked.

"Yes. Although before I can suggest what he might do about the situation, he's got to see it as a problem. I wonder what makes it so automatic for him to think that he can be responsible for everyone else."

We went on to talk about the pattern of *doing for* the Hebrew people what they could do for themselves—of a few being responsible *for* them, whether the few were slave masters or Moses and Aaron. He said maybe we'd had slave masters for so long that we'd forgotten how to make our own decisions. And that everyone must become aware of what's at stake. "Thank you for helping me think this through," he said, as he got up to leave. *That* is a leader.

Yours for leaders,
Kezi

Entry 8.6
A humble guy
Exod 18:14–27

Dear Diary,

Jethro talked with Moses about making some changes here. Not only that—Moses listened. He followed Jethro's guidance entirely, dividing us up into groups and setting up a process for each group to work out its own challenges.

It's not surprising to me that he took Jethro's advice. He was like this when he was little, too, listening for what others thought instead of thinking he knew what to do. I always thought it was because Miriam was bringing him back and forth a lot, from the palace to Jochebed, during the years their mother was nursing him. A little guy having to go back and forth between two worlds so different would learn fast that he was *not* the center of things and that he needed to attend to what was happening around him.

At the time I thought he would outgrow that tentativeness. It still shows up, though, in his halting speech and in positive ways too. He continues to be interested—genuinely interested—in what others think, taking time to understand different views before he takes his own position. I think he likes being out here with a chance to try something new. Still, he remains one humble guy.

Noticing more,
Kezi

Entry 8.7
Seekers' Council—Kezi, presenter
1 Chr 4:17

Introduction

What a different setting for this Council meeting, compared to the last time I presented back in Egypt! We have more to do, but we have come a long way. Usually, I include many generations in a family chart, but in this case, I have been unable to get clear facts. The lack of knowledge may be a cost of our enslavement.

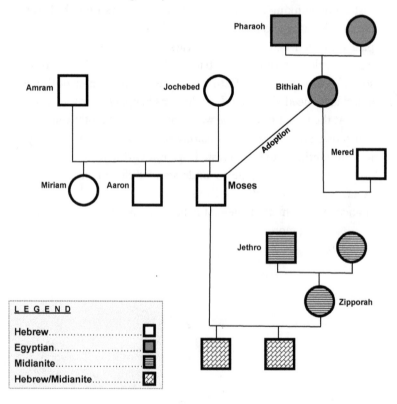

Figure 8. Family ties. **The chart shows four different ethnic backgrounds in the family of Moses. Moses was the youngest of three children. His father, Amram, was a descendant of Jacob's son Levi, but little more is known about**

previous generations. Moses was adopted as a baby, with Princess Bithiah, an Egyptian, as his adoptive mother. While he was raised in the palace, he stayed in contact with his birth family. He married a Midianite, Zipporah, and had two sons with her. His adoptive mother, Princess Bithiah, recently married a Hebrew, Mered.

Concerns and questions

Miriam, the oldest of Jochebed's children, has said that while she remembers her grandparents, she remembers no one ever talking about their family lineage. I have encouraged her to ask around about this, but so far, she has not. How unusual is it for people not to know their ancestry? Or for them to avoid asking family members about the details? The work of knowing one's family background is harder, I think, than it looks.

More generally, I am interested in how her family is doing. All of us are facing many challenges. With Miriam, though, and her brothers, what might I be missing that would be useful in their roles as leaders of our people?

Council comments by topic

1. Family lineage

Kezi, I think the lack of information on the family lineage is a possible "tell" of a lot of avoiding or perhaps even cutoff between generations of family members. On the other hand, as you say, the years of slavery have made information hard to come by. In any event, whenever I notice cutoff in the past, I usually find that people have trouble maintaining connections in the present. Would you say that's true of this family?

2. Intense closeness

I am interested in Miriam's description of being so close to her mother that she knew automatically what her mother would want her to do. It is more than a strong connection. It is more like the two people—mother and child—never separate.

Does that pattern continue even after the death of one's mother—does the child (adult child, that is), continue to "know" and do what her mother would want? In what ways is that behavior limiting or unrealistic? Is separating from one's parents a lifelong project?

3. Contact with family members

Speaking for myself, the most useful thing I ever did was get to know my mother after I grew up and had my own children. It wasn't only that I spent more time with her. I also spent more time with her brother, and his wife, and many others who had known her. Then I started to get a more realistic view of my mother.

Now, without our slave masters, we have more opportunities to be around our family members. Maybe too many! In what ways is the increased togetherness out here in the desert creating its own difficulties?

4. Adoption

What impact did the adoption of Moses by Bithiah have on the relationship of Moses with his birth mother, Jochebed? Did his more complicated upbringing reflect or create some flexibility in him? In his family? How did the arrangement impact his siblings? His triangles with his parents? What difference has it made in his ability to become a leader?

5. Resourcefulness

Jethro's place on the family chart is important. Moses himself has a high regard for his father-in-law, which has been useful to us as a people. Jethro knows a lot more about living in this environment than any of us.

In what ways can we use him—and Moses's wife, Zipporah, too, for that matter—to manage ourselves out here in the desert? What should we be asking them about? To me, the narrow focus of slavery, of only doing what one is told, of asking no questions, continues to get in our way now. How do we get organized out here? Beyond survival, what matters to us?

6. Pain

Pain has accumulated among our people. The experience of being enslaved has been passed down through many generations. It sounds so obvious, but it took getting away before I could look back and see it.

While pain itself isn't passed down—I don't feel the whip on my grandmother's back—still, the results of pain are passed down. The fear and the bitterness, along with the strength to endure, spread through families and down the generations. Our inheritance.

What do we do with all this accumulated pain? How does it damage our capacity to face our challenges? What did the generations above us do to cope with enslavement, to manage the pain, both physical and emotional? What patterns are no longer useful to us now? How do we heal, as individuals, as families, and as a people?

9

Families Growing Up

Entry 9.1
Principles
Exod 19–20

Dear Diary,

We've been in the wilderness for only a few months, but it seems like years. Every day is difficult. Something is happening now, though, something that may make it easier to live out here. Moses has been up on Mount Sinai, and there were terrible storms while he was gone. When he came back, he said the LORD had spoken to him in the clouds.

It's what the LORD said, though, that matters. Moses came back with a set of rules that he read to us. We all shouted that we would follow these commandments. It came as a relief—people were ready for them. We all understood that we had to find a path together, that we had to agree on some rules. There has been too much chaos, too much not knowing what to do. Ever since Jethro was here, we've been talking about how we want to live. It is good to get clear.

Mered and I talked about how powerful the day had been. Diary, I have never in my life seen thunder and lightning like that. And Moses, well, he was a different person than I've ever seen him be. Anyhow, we talked for a while about how it had happened before Mered turned his attention to the list of rules Moses had given us. "What did you think about them? Anything new?" he asked, smiling.

"For sure," I said, with a laugh. "Take the first commandment, *You shall have no other gods before me.* That's new. I don't know what it means, though. I don't know the LORD as Moses does. The LORD has never spoken to me from a burning bush."

"Interesting. Maybe that's the point." He thought for a minute. "Are the new rules consistent with your own principles?"

"Well," I said, in a voice as halting as Moses, for it was hard to figure out what I *did* think, "Well, some are the same as in Egypt. Stealing, for instance, could get you in trouble. And yes, I'd say that one is consistent with my own thinking. Another one I agree with, one that was different from Egypt, is the ban on idol worship. I used to watch that, back at the palace. How far from reality, to think that bowing to a hand-carving might matter. What a waste of time!"

"You thought it looked silly," he said.

"I did think it was silly. It meant something to them, though, I could see that much." I went on. "A rule that's important to me is not taking the LORD's name in vain. When people start swearing, they are letting their feelings take over. I am glad for my feelings, but I try not to let them run my life or ruin my day." Then I stopped. These new commandments were more interesting than I had realized. "What do you think, Mered?"

"I think they are brilliant. I think these rules can guide a person in how to both enjoy the togetherness of a group and be an individual self. When one person finds a way to be more of an individual without distancing from others, others find the freedom to become who they are going to become too. The whole group matures." He stopped. "Does this make sense to you?"

"Yes," I answered, which was a lie and probably breaking a commandment. I was still thinking about principles. I don't think I ever realized before how important it is to *have* principles. It's one thing for Moses to lay down some rules. It's another thing for each of us to *want* to live by them. Not my problem, though, right?

What I see here is opportunity—questions I can ask others about what matters to them and who they are trying to become.

As he left, I asked after Bithiah. Guess what? She's pregnant!

Your delighted diarist,

Kezi

Entry 9.2
Fury
Exod 32, 35; Num 3:1–15

Dear Diary,

As always, I guess, things get worse after they get better. Moses went back up the mountain to get more instructions from the LORD. He stayed gone so long that the people got afraid and started pressuring Aaron to build an idol for them. So, Aaron had them bring jewelry. He melted it down and built a golden calf, which some began to worship.

Moses was furious when he got back. Furious with Aaron, and mad at all of us. Before it was over, the Levites—remember, Aaron and Moses come from the family of Levi—gathered around Moses and Aaron, and killed over three thousand people, blaming them for the idols. It was a terrible thing. And it has set us back as a people, back into immaturity and just plain fear.

In the end, the Levites came out of it as the winners, seen (by many) as on the side of the LORD. They have been proclaimed as the priests for our people, forever. Well, really?

I saw what Aaron was up against when Moses was gone. The people were so upset without Moses around that Aaron had to do something. I don't fault him for that. He's always looking for a way to keep everyone happy, that's just Aaron. But the idea that he should be high priest, that he and his sons should dress in fancy robes, and parade around the rest of us, I wonder whether Aaron's not taking advantage of the situation for his own gain. I have little patience for this kind of thing, and even less now.

I see already that what I've just written is all wrong. Aaron's not to blame either. The vestments and all the other things—the tabernacle, the ark to hold the tablets of the Ten Commandments, the lampstand, all being made now—all these things will work to keep the people calm. They are worth it, I suppose, if people can't manage themselves.

Your disappointed diarist,
Kezi

Entry 9.3
Nobody's slave
Exod 35:1–3

Dear Diary,

Moses talked to us all today, in the most serious of terms, about keeping a Sabbath rest. After what just happened, with over three thousand people dead, his announcement that anyone working on the Sabbath will be put to death was met with a grim nod from the people. Right now, the Sabbath seems like another thing to be afraid of, to get right. But I don't think that was the intention, nor how it's going to end. I think we are all going to start looking forward to it. After spending our lives as slaves, having to work every day, we are free to take it easy. One day every week. I intend to keep this rule.

Your no-longer-a-slave diarist,

Kezi

Entry 9.4
Ordinary lives
Num 11:1–30

Dear Diary,

We have broken camp from Sinai now, and moving on has been very difficult. Wandering around a desert is not an easy business. Water is scarce. Manna is meh. There are snakes out here, lots of snakes. People are getting really frustrated.

Apparently, Moses has gotten tired of all the complaining and has directed all seventy elders to join him tomorrow at the tent of meeting. Two of the elders—Eldad and Medad—came by to talk with me about it. They both have work to do in the camp that would keep them from attending the meeting. What should they do?

"The work you need to do back at camp, is it your responsibility?" I asked. They both nodded yes. "Is it important to you as a person, does it matter to you that you are the one who does it?" Again, they each said yes. "How do you understand the first commandment, to have no other gods before the LORD? Does it speak to this situation?" I asked.

Eldad spoke first. "I think it means to do what the LORD has given me to do, regardless of what anyone else wants or needs from me."

"I will be staying behind at the camp tomorrow to do my work." Medad added.

They both got up, thanked me for helping them think it through, and left.

Later, I heard about what happened. Out at the tent of meeting, when Moses began to speak as a prophet, all the elders with him also began to prophesy. Not only that, but back in the camp, Eldad and Medad did also. When a young man ran out to the tent to tell Moses what was happening, Joshua (more and more, Moses's right-hand man) implored Moses to have them stopped from prophesying. Moses quickly ended all talk of that.

"Are you jealous for my sake?" Moses asked. "Would that all the Lord's people were prophets and that the Lord would put his spirit on them!"

The situation reminded me of something Moses said before he went up on Mount Sinai, that the Lord had told him that we were to become a kingdom of priests. For that to be possible, at least as I see it, each of us must honor the work of our ordinary lives, as Medad and Eldad did.

Anywhere that a person does what matters to him, does he— or she—become holy in the doing of it? I think of my friend Phari back in Egypt, who tried so hard to do her work just so. I still miss her. I wonder if she is okay, and if she is part of a kingdom of priests. Who knows how the Lord might work?

The opposite might be true also. Whenever a person sacrifices what they are called to do to accommodate or to please someone else, they start to lose their own self, their own being. That's what happened to us as slaves, and now we must learn another way.

Yours for another way,

Kezi

Entry 9.5
Friendship
Num 12, 1 Chr 4:17b

Dear Diary,

Today I heard that Miriam had been banished from the camp due to a skin condition—possibly contagious. She was tossed out for seven days. Well, I got my canteen, filled it with water, and crept away to see her. There are strict rules about not visiting those who have been banished from camp. But there was no way I was not going to check on her.

When I found her, she was hidden on the shady side of a rock—less likely for a snake to be over on that side and more comfortable for her. I knew a cave nearby and took her there right away. She looked pale and troubled.

After I gave her some water, we began to talk. She told me how she and Aaron had gotten mad at Moses over his Cushite wife. Really, they were angry about how the LORD always seemed to prefer Moses to them. Before she knew it, her skin had broken out. Aaron had pleaded with Moses, who had pleaded with the LORD, that she be healed. And she was. But still, the weeklong exile had to be imposed.

I sighed. "You suffer, while your brothers have it easier."

"Yes. But no matter now. I'm going to die out here, alone. You all will be moving on, and I will lack the strength to follow."

"No. That's *not* what's going to happen. The people have refused to break camp until you come back. We are waiting for you before we set out."

She smiled. It wasn't much of a smile, still, she got it. She realized that everyone understands her importance. Actions speak—and a whole community refusing to move on says something.

"Before I go back today, there is one more thing. Guess who had her baby?"

Miriam shrugged.

"Bithiah," I said. "And guess what she and Mered named their firstborn child?"

Miriam looked puzzled.

"Miriam."

Then we both cried. We wept buckets.

Your diarist,

Kezi

Entry 9.6
Letting go
Num 20:1–13

Dear Diary,

It's been a tough time for me. We came to the wilderness of Zin, every bit as unpleasant as it sounds, when Miriam died. My best friend forever in this life, gone. I am trying hard to be brave about it, as she was all those years ago when the palace guards took her away. Ah, Miriam, my friend, how I will miss you.

That's not all though. When we found water at Meribah, Moses and Aaron got a little carried away, acting like they had made it come out of the rock instead of giving the LORD the credit. Rumor is, the LORD has told them that they will pay a price—that they will die here, in the desert. That Joshua will take us across the Jordan and into the land we've been promised.

Well, let's face it. None of our generation is going to make it to the promised land—that much is increasingly clear—and it's time to start thinking about how to continue our work. I wonder about the family of Joshua. And Caleb too. They are emerging as the younger leaders these days. Who in their families might become a Seeker?

Yours for letting go,
Kezi

Entry 9.7
Snakebit
Num 21:1–9

Dear Diary,

Everyone was already tired and discouraged from traveling around and getting nowhere, when our latest desert setting came complete with a snake infestation. Lots of people have been bitten, and some have died. Moses made a bronze serpent, stuck it on a pole, and told people to stare at it if they wanted to live. I thought this was an odd thing, and way too much like an idol for my own tastes. Still, that's what Moses did, and now, people have stopped dying!

All along, I have been visiting those who were bitten. Those who lived have told me that they liked staring at the pole. They say things like "It calms me down" or "I don't worry as long as I'm looking at it."

You don't suppose, Diary, that it's not the snakebite itself that kills but the fear, combined with the poison, that's fatal? I remember once—another life ago, it seems, when Moses was little—I was sitting at the edge of the Nile, watching him play and splash, when a snake swam by. If there's anything scarier than a live serpent with its jaws open, looking straight at you, inches away, I'd like to know what that is. I got up and got him out of there *so* fast! I don't know if I've ever been more afraid.

Of course, now, people are already afraid—afraid that we are stuck here, that we will never find our way out of the desert. The bronze serpent on the pole has worked to take away the helplessness, the sense that nothing could be done, at least about snakes. Maybe that's its real value.

There are other things, though, that people have been saying. "I keep staring at the bronze serpent because Moses said it would make me better" or "because Moses said the Lord said it would make me better." These answers trouble me. They sound too close to idol worship, to me, too much like the Egyptians and their panoply of false gods. I do not think it is what the Lord—the same

LORD who gave us the Ten Commandments—would have us do or become.

Still, the serpent on the pole makes sense to me. For people to face their fear and get over something, I think they must live with it—or stare at it—for a while. When we first came out to the wilderness, I was so afraid of heights, I had trouble hiking up the steep hills out here. Now I can do it, no problem. I might still get a bit dizzy, but it doesn't scare me anymore.

Maybe we as a people had to learn how to manage our fears. Maybe that's what the wilderness was for. Maybe we are almost ready to move on.

Almost ready,
Kezi

Entry 9.8
Purpose
Exod 19:6

Dear Diary,

Mered came by this morning and plunged right into his latest idea. "I've been watching us out here in the desert, starting to form as a people, able to work together, and to agree on our own rules. Do you think we've changed?"

We talked about the simplistic, blaming attitudes many had when we left Egypt. Are we growing up, as individuals and families and as a people? The Ten Commandments came up, both as a way of guiding family and individual behavior and as a way of distinguishing ourselves from others.

"It's more than whether we've changed," I said. "Do you see us developing a purpose? Without a goal, we're still floundering around, even if we've learned how to organize ourselves a bit."

"When Moses first went up on Mount Sinai, he came down talking about how we were to become a kingdom of priests and a holy nation," Mered said. "At the time, I did not get it at all. Maybe that's our purpose—to live a different way, without idols, and according to the commandments."

"That is quite a purpose," I said. I smiled, a bit of a sad smile, as I thought about the difference between the goal and the current reality. There was nothing more to say.

Your more realistic diarist,

Kezi

Entry 9.9
Seekers' Council—Kezi, presenter
Num 12, Exod 4:27–31

Introduction

I have known Miriam, Aaron, and Moses, for my entire life. The three of them did not always get along, of course, when we were children. I am interested in exploring how their triangle worked. All three served as leaders on our journey our of Egypt.

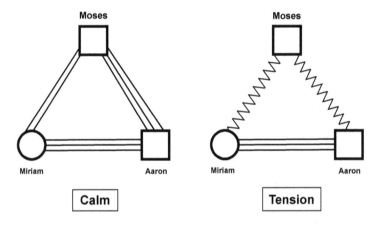

Figure 9. Triangles. **Relationships among Moses, Aaron, and Miriam are displayed during a period of calm and during a time of increased tension. The triangle between the three siblings seems to have worked with the middle child having the strongest connection to each of the others. During periods of relative calm, all three were able to stay in good contact with one another. (Left triangle: three lines between Aaron and Miriam, and Aaron and Moses; two lines between Miriam and Moses.) Under increasing stress, Miriam and Aaron sided against Moses (jagged lines from Aaron to Moses and from Miriam to Moses, three lines connecting Miriam to Aaron).**

Concerns and questions

Today I would like to focus on leadership. Moses, Aaron, and Miriam were our leaders in this journey. Now, with Miriam's death, it seems important to stop and think about how she and her brothers worked together. What can we learn? What did the triangle between the siblings have to do with leadership?

Council comments by topic

1. Closeness

Kezi, first, I want to offer my condolences on the loss of your lifelong friend, Miriam. She has been an important part of our lives. What would you say were her greatest strengths? How would she have described her relationship with her brothers in their early years? In what ways did her position as the oldest, as responsible for her brothers, continue past their childhood? How would she have seen it? More generally, how do you see Miriam as a leader among us?

2. Firstborn sons

Although Aaron was the middle child, he was also the first male child of his parents. I wonder whether Aaron, from childhood, was close to his father, and how the triangle with his father and brother might have worked. What was it like for Aaron to be the representative of Moses with Pharaoh? How does the closeness of Aaron and Moses make it easier for them to work together? Does it ever make it harder?

3. Birth order

I am interested in the birth order of these three siblings. Aaron as the middle child might be the one most aware of the other two—or maybe, the one paying the most attention to how the group is getting along. Any tension between Miriam and Moses, he'd know about it. How does that awareness make a difference in the triangle? Did it impact flexibility—the ability of all three members to use each other as resources when needed?

4. Challenges

How were the challenges of life different for Moses, Aaron, and Miriam? In what ways were their lives the same? Different? How did their lives shape each of them for what they had to do? As children, Miriam and Aaron were together for many years before the birth of Moses. And then, the time Moses spent at the palace would have meant less time with his siblings. How might these realities have altered their triangle?

4. Anxiety

The increasing tension among our people, as we continue to wander around the desert, is easy to see and almost feel. I wonder, when the three of them were children, how the anxiety worked. If one were upset, would the others know? How would they manage? How did tension spread through the sibling triangle and the interlocking triangles with their parents and others? I think their ability to lead us as a people depended a lot on how they had grown up, with a capacity to work together that had become finely tuned, over the years.

5. Maturity

Families are better off when the most mature members are leading. No one wants a two-year-old in charge. Sometimes as a people, it has seemed to me that the least mature—the ones doing the most complaining—are running things.

To what extent have our leaders managed to change things? How did they do it? In what ways are we still stuck, still expecting others to tell us what to do?

10

Navigating New Terrain

Entry 10.1
Too agreeable
Josh 1–3, 6, 15:13–19

Dear Diary,

Joshua's visit yesterday prompted me to sit down and write about the years since we crossed the Jordan into the promised land. Finally. I have been meaning to write for years.

Who am I? Oh, of course. I am Achsah, named after the daughter of Caleb, who was my mother's closest friend. Both my mother and Auntie Asch loved the land and delighted in cultivating it.

I am one of the lesser Seekers, for sure. I know, it is unwise for me to compare myself to anyone. I don't, usually, and it doesn't bother me at all to be myself. I just wanted you to know who I am. I'm like my mother—less interested in writing or talking than in working the land—and I have spent most of my life gardening.

People came here to see my auntie for counsel, and now they come to me. The Seekers took me in, I think mostly out of pity at first, for myself and the people who came to see me. They have taught me well. And one thing that I myself offer is a capacity to stay calm when others are tense. People come here to figure out what to do with their tension and their troubles.

One more thing they come for—the land. My auntie picked a great spot. We live in the most beautiful area a person could imagine, lush, with grasses and trees and birds and other creatures. It is healing to be here. Peaceful. I always suggest that visitors stay a while.

These years have been difficult. The first thing that happened after we crossed the Jordan was based on the work of spies who'd gone in ahead of us. They'd discovered the town of Jericho and met a woman, Rahab, who cooperated with them. Long story short, we surrounded the city, blowing trumpets and raising a loud crashing sound, and they—the entire town—surrendered. What happened next? Well, we destroyed them. Killed every man, woman, child, and beast—with the single exception of Rahab and her extended family.

I've heard my mother and Auntie Asch talk about Jericho many times, saying that the LORD had told Joshua to do this. I wonder. Of course, moving here meant that sometimes we'd have to show force to take territory. But would the same LORD who gave us the law—the Ten Commandments we all know by heart—would that same LORD have required this destruction? Down to the donkeys? It makes no sense to me.

When Joshua and I started talking, I decided to ask him how he thought about the destruction of Jericho. He said that in his view, the LORD had asked him to be a military leader, with all that was involved. He got a little heated at first, but then, when I stayed neutral, he managed to regain his own capacity to take a different view from mine. Calmly. That's what I was after. He needs—we all need—the ability to disagree while staying in contact with each other. The important thing is to be mature enough to talk about different views.

I do not think that the job of the Seekers is to agree, necessarily, with those who come for counsel. Being overly agreeable is not necessarily a good thing. People start losing the ability to think for themselves, and if there's anything that our years in the wilderness taught us, it's that we need thinking people to be strong. Too much agreement is like becoming slaves again.

Your new diarist,

Achsah

Entry 10.2
Just asking
Judg 3:1–6

Dear Diary,

Joshua came back today to talk about idol worship. The local gods—Baal and Astarte—are thought by the local people to help crops to grow. And now that we have settled in and started doing more farming, more of the Hebrew people are bowing to the local idols.

"Wasn't it only a matter of time before people started trying them out? Seeing if they work? People will do almost anything when life gets hard," I said.

"Well, maybe, but Moses would have called the people out for it. He would have made them stop, I know he would have," Joshua said.

I could hear the urgency in his voice, the pressure he felt to be like Moses. I pictured the triangles: Joshua, Moses, and any other person. "What difference did it make, when Moses told the people what to do?" I asked.

"Not much, really. I mean, they didn't change, except maybe for a few days, then it was back to business as usual. The complaints about the food, for instance—almost nonstop. Telling them what to do never worked. What was worse was that then they expected him to keep on telling them what to do."

"Sort of like we were still slaves, just a different master?"

"Well, yeah. Sometimes, you have to give orders. Men in battle, who don't know the whole picture, must be told what their part is and how to do it. Most of the time, though, you want people to think for themselves. It is too much for the leader to be responsible for everyone all the time."

"What was the Lord trying to do with the ten rules? I have wondered about that many times. Was the Lord telling us what to do?" I asked.

"I had not ever thought about it that way," he said, and then he got up and started pacing the cave floor. Then he said, "Children have to be told what to do. But does the LORD want children, or does the LORD want us to grow up? After childhood, people must decide for themselves whether they want to follow the commandments, and how they will lead their lives. Each of us gets to decide what god or idols to serve."

"Thank you for today. I wish you long life and much wisdom in your work," he added. I must have helped, somehow. All I did was ask some questions.

Just asking,
Achsah

Entry 10.3
Decide for yourself
Josh 24

Dear Diary,

Joshua got in front of everyone today, looking much older than he did just last week. He reviewed our history and the recent tendency towards idol worship. He urged them to decide—to choose—which gods they would serve. "But as for me and my house," he added, "we will serve the LORD."

It was amazing to watch the response. People stepped up to the challenge, declaring that they, too, would serve the LORD. They looked thrilled, absolutely thrilled, to be invited to think for themselves. It was like stepping into a grove of trees on a hot day. The atmosphere was totally different, fresh and cool.

Will it last? Well, of course not, right? We are human beings, after all. But I still think giving people a choice, rather than telling them what to do, is worth its weight in gold. I wish you could have been there to see it.

Yours for freedom,
Achsah

Entry 10.4

Signs

Judg 2:6–16, 6:1–27

Dear Diary,

We buried Joshua, a true servant of the LORD, in the hill country of Ephraim, north of Mount Ga-ash. Our people have continued to find our way in this new land, with leaders arising when a situation requires it. The Amalekites and the Midianites oppress us. There are some who look to other gods and some who look to the LORD. Nothing new and nothing worth writing about.

Today, though, something new happened to me. I had a visit from a young man named Gideon. Seems that he was beating wheat out of a wine press (standard way of hiding the food, so the Midianites do not take it) when an angel visited him. As Gideon tells it, an angel appeared to him and said something about his being a mighty warrior.

"A mighty warrior," I said, trying to repress a smile. People are always coming to me with these things the LORD said to them, and I am thinking *really?* This time, though, Gideon was completely in my corner.

"Yes. I thought it was very strange and I told him so. I mean, the people I come from were not mighty warriors by any stretch of the imagination. My family is the weakest of all of them."

"How would you measure that?" I wondered aloud.

"That's easy. We are about to starve to death. I mean, we have almost nothing, beyond a bit of land at Ophrah. Other branches of our family are at least surviving, and they help us some. We are the least capable of any of them."

"What did you tell the angel?" I asked. It was important to me to understand how he had described himself to this character, whether imaginary or real. I was trying hard to hear him out.

"I asked for a sign. I figured, if I'm being commissioned—and that's what the angel said, can you imagine—if so, then I need some physical sign that I'm not seeing things."

Well, here was more awareness than I expected. Gideon himself realized that he sounded delusional, that maybe he'd worked in the hot sun too long. He wasn't so much testing the LORD as assuring himself he'd heard right. "What happened then?"

"I made some food, as the angel asked. I put it on a rock, and a fire came up and consumed it. And the LORD said *Peace*. He said more, though, telling me to destroy an altar of Baal."

"That's . . . quite a tall order."

"It is. And I am afraid. My own family may kill me for this, for, as you know, it is my father's altar. And the townspeople, too, will be angry—many people worship there."

I asked him whether it was realistic that his father or some other locals would kill him. I tried to make the question as bland as possible—he needed to be able to think clearly about the risks, and how was I to know how intense his father was and what might happen?

"Well, my father is more or less a fan of Baal, depending on how well the crops are doing. He comes and goes on the idol worship. He and I have never been close, really, but I don't think he'd hurt me. Would he stand up for me? I kind of doubt it. And there's a lot of local sentiment around worshiping Baal."

Then I asked what *he* thought about it and what he wanted to do. He said that if the local people found out that he was taking the altar down, they would stop him, he was sure of that. He's a cautious sort, aware of what can go wrong. Presumably the LORD would have known that, in selecting him as a leader. It will be interesting to see what happens.

Your curious diarist,
Achsah

Entry 10.5
Father and son
Judg 6:28–40

Dear Diary,

Gideon waited until dark and took down the Baal altar. Then he built another and sacrificed one of his father's bulls there. The next morning, the people cried out against him, but his father, Joash, took Gideon's side, saying, "If Baal is a god, let him contend for himself!"

"I was stunned," Gideon said. "I had always worked for my father and followed his lead. And then, there he was, following mine. I did not know, if I were in the LORD's corner, whether my father would join me there or not. But I led and he followed. It took courage for both of us," he added, with some gentle wonderment.

"Do you ever remember doing this before? Taking a position, I mean, knowing that family members might disagree?"

"Yes, now that you say it that way, I have. With my brothers, sometimes, and with my mother. Never before with my father. This is new. And it is making me a different person. It is not just that he took my side. I mean, that mattered—it may have kept me alive or at least in one piece. But it's more than that. We are equals now—somehow, standing up for my own beliefs changed everything."

"You are now no longer a child. It made you an adult in relationship to your father. At least, it did for a moment, and it seems to have stuck."

He nodded. "Yes, that's how it appears. I am surprised at myself. And at him."

"Do you think it will be easier or harder the next time you see something differently from others in your family?"

"Easier, I think. It will take practice in going ahead and saying what's on my mind, but it has started now."

"What's next?" I asked.

"With my father, I don't know. I do know that I am ready to lead our people, not just the young among us, but all of us."

And now, Diary, our enemies are gathering in a nearby valley, while Gideon is rounding up our allies from the region. Everyone is terrified. Gideon, the same cautious guy, set up some tests to know that the LORD is with him—putting a dry fleece on the threshing floor and asking for a small miracle—that in the morning, there be no dew on the floor but dew on the fleece. It happened. The next day, he asked for the opposite, which also happened.

I asked Gideon how he dared to ask—twice—for the LORD to give him signs. He said that he asked the LORD not to be angry that he needed evidence before proceeding. He talked about it as though it were a logical request. He said he would not put his own and other people's lives at risk without doing what he could to ascertain that all would be well.

He is very clear about the importance of caution, and maybe it's the right thing to do here. I don't know. Many Hebrew people maintain a certain vigilance towards threat, a vestige of our many years of slavery and deprivation, as I see it. Can vigilance itself be passed down in families from generation to generation? I wonder.

And I wonder if I'm making a difference. Was Gideon's first decision to tear down the altar to Baal based partly on our conversation? Was this second one, to defend us against the encroaching armies, an outgrowth of what we'd discussed? Would he have done the same without me? Maybe. Probably. Whatever my small part, I'm glad I was there for him to talk to. Leaders need people to think with.

Your thought partner,
Achsah

Entry 10.6
Family decision
Judg 8:22–28

Dear Diary,

Gideon came to me this morning—looking much older these days—and wanting to talk about his legacy. We have had many years of peace under his leadership. He's been getting pressure, not only to become our ruler but to set things up so that his son and grandson will rule after he dies. He said to me that the LORD has said nothing to him on the subject—such a contrast to other times—and that he was unclear about the best path.

Then, he told me about a battle he'd led where the LORD had been quite clear about what to do. "The LORD told me to cut the number of troops, first from twenty-two thousand to ten thousand, and then down to three hundred."

"What happened?" I asked.

"Well, we beat them with trumpets and crashing glass, confusing everyone in the camp. They fought with each other for a bit, and then threw down their swords and ran."

"How do you understand what happened? What sense do you make of it?"

"The LORD won. It was not our strength, that's for sure. I remember thinking at the time that somehow everyone should look to the LORD, and not depend too much on others."

We talked about how Joshua handled things at the end of his life, giving people both ownership of and responsibility for their own choices. This was enough for Gideon. He started talking about each person looking to the LORD, being responsible for oneself and to others. He went on and on about wanting his son and grandson to be free to lead their own lives, without responsibilities for others. He left, knowing that he would decline the chance to rule. He said he would remind everyone that they didn't need a person to rule them—that they had the LORD.

Yours with nothing to add,
Achsah

Entry 10.7
Parting
Ruth 1:1–3

Dear Diary,

Today I face a difficult time. My dear friend, my closest companion, Naomi, has come by to talk with me about leaving Judah. She, her husband, and their two sons are going. The famine has brought us to this as a people, doing whatever we can to survive. I stay behind, ever-so-slightly better off, due to my family's land. It is not enough to feed others, and Naomi, of course, already knew this.

She put it to me quite simply. "We'll starve if we stay. And I have heard that there is food in Moab."

Moab, land founded by the incestuous offspring of Lot and his older daughter. I guess I know a hundred jokes about Moabites, and they are always good for a laugh. Well, not so much now. And I said as much. It never works to ridicule others. In the end, the lack of respect always comes back on oneself.

"Yes, it will be hard to go there, especially at first. And yet, if we can find work there, we can survive. That's all that matters now. After all, we have two sons."

Ah, two sons. She has been so proud of them. That's what is giving her the strength to move on.

"What do you think your sons will learn from going there?" I asked.

"Not to be helpless. To face whatever challenge is ahead," she said, not missing a beat in answering me.

So she is gone. Now I must be brave, too, in my own way. May Naomi find food for her family, and wives for her sons, and prosperity for herself in all she does!

Your sad but realistic diarist,

Achsah

Entry 10.8

Resourcefulness

Ruth 1:4–22

Dear Diary,

What terrible times we live in. Naomi is back. Her husband died first. Then both of her sons married, and then both sons died, without leaving any children. One of the daughters-in-law, Orpah, went back to her own family. The other, Ruth, refused to go back to her kin, choosing to stay with Naomi and journey here together. Thank goodness. I shudder to think of what might have happened to Naomi if she had tried to travel back alone.

And, of course, everyone is talking about how sad it all is. This is what people do when they are afraid. They find someone else to share all the details with and feel better as they spread their own fears around. Well, it's hardly a time to criticize others. For my part, I have found Naomi and Ruth a place to sleep. And to-day—while Ruth was off, looking for food—Naomi and I had time to talk.

"Don't call me Naomi anymore," she said. "I only answer to *Mara*—bitter—for the LORD has brought me home empty and bitter."

"Ah. Mara. Who can fault you for your bitterness," I said. Inside, my mind was working fast. Sometimes, saying a feeling aloud can help a person to cope with it, to reflect on it. Then the feeling is less overwhelming to them, and they can begin to think again.

Sometimes, though, a continued focus on a feeling sends a person down a rabbit hole from which they cannot return. It can bind them up, keeping them all the more stuck. What would be useful now? How do I be a friend?

We talked for a bit about all that had happened. I tried to ask some simple, factual questions, to engage her mind. Then I took a chance on her capacity to get clear about herself.

"I remember your courage when you left us. You were un-complaining as you journeyed away, far from home, to a land and a people completely alien to us," I said.

"And yet, they were not so alien. Really, you should have been there. My sons found lovely wives, both of them. I still think of Orpah, and I hope all is well with her. Now, though, I must turn my attention to Ruth."

I smiled to myself. The same old Naomi. Always thinking of her family, always finding a way. Better build on that, before the bitterness sweeps her away again.

"What would it look like, to be resourceful now? Where would you start?" I wondered.

"I've been thinking about Boaz," she said. "My husband was related to him. And Ruth told me that yesterday, while she was gleaning in his fields, he had taken an interest in her. Maybe he's a way forward." And so she talked on about her plans for Ruth and Boaz. As I listened to her plans, I heard her becoming free from *mara*.

Your hopeful diarist,
Achsah

Entry 10.9

Mara is gone

Ruth 2–4

Dear Diary,

Amazing news today. Boaz has married Ruth. *Mara* is gone, Naomi is back. I am going to invite her to come with me to the next Seekers' Council. We'll be talking about her family's story, and it may be useful to have her there.

Your happy diarist,

Achsah

Entry 10.10 Seekers' Council—Achsah, presenter, with guest Naomi

Introduction

I am happy to welcome my old and dear friend Naomi to our Council today.

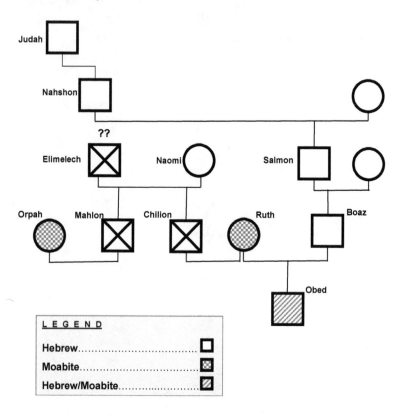

Figure 10. The family of Ruth and Boaz. **Naomi and her husband and two sons left Bethlehem during a famine, settling in Moab, where the sons married. Naomi's husband died, and then her two sons, who were childless, died (notated by *x*'s). Naomi decided to return home to Bethlehem, and Ruth, one of her daughters-in-law, chose to accompany her. Ruth has recently married Boaz, a descendant of Jacob's son Judah and kin to Naomi's husband, Elimelech. How Elimelech and Boaz were related is unclear (notated by ??).**

Concerns and questions

I have been friends with Naomi for many years. I have watched the early years with her two sons, their difficult decision to move to Moab, and now her return with her daughter-in-law Ruth. I wonder, what can we learn from this family? Given the question, I decided to include Naomi in our Council gathering today.

Council comments by topic

1. Challenges

Thank you, Achsah. And welcome, Naomi, we are glad to have you join our conversation.

I'm thinking about how Naomi managed to engage the challenges of her life. What makes some people able to step up to difficult times, while others tend to get helpless in similar circumstances? During the forty years in the wilderness, how might Naomi's family have met their challenges? Had the family's experience over time somehow created a capacity in her to face her own troubles?

2. Emotions

I am interested in hearing more about Achsah's approach to Naomi's renaming herself *Mara*, or bitter. It seems like a risky approach, in some ways. What difference do you think it made to her, when you chose to use her new name?

3. Relationships

What struck me was the importance of relationships. Naomi by herself seems like a completely different thing from Naomi concerned about her sons or Naomi concerned about her daughters-in-law. How much of our sense of self is who we are in relationship to others?

4. Group hatred

I wonder about the Hebrew people and their hatred of the Moabites. It cannot have been easy for Naomi to go to Moab, nor for Ruth to have traveled back here. I imagine they've been somewhat protected by Boaz. Still, this cannot have been easy.

I wonder if Naomi has any thoughts or insight to bring to the subject of our hatred of the Moabites. It must have been something she gave a lot of thought to, while she lived there.

5. Naomi's response

On the way to Moab, I was scared. I had heard so many bad things about the Moabites that it was hard to be realistic about what might happen. Yes, there was a famine at home, where we would starve if we stayed, but what would happen to us in Moab? Fear and dread and confusion were taking over.

One night, my husband, my sons, and I climbed a steep ridge and camped at the top. We heard jackals below us and went to look. Usually, you know, they live as pairs, and chase off any other jackals coming into their territory. That night, though, a pack of them had come together to hunt down their prey. I guessed that they were hungry, just like us. I thought, well, if jackals can manage to cooperate so that everyone can eat, surely people can too. It changed my whole view. Next morning, I got up, squared my shoulders, and headed out, determined to make a go of it.

I won't say the Moabites were the same as us. Sometimes yes, and sometimes no. They had different ways of doing things and, sometimes, different ways of thinking about things. Their perspectives were interesting. My life is better for having known them and for having lived there.

After we had lived in Moab for a while, I was surprised to find that they had as many jokes about us as we had about them. I wondered, what is the habit of making fun of other people about? Is it everywhere? How does it begin?

I thought back to my own boys, when they were young, and how they would cry if a stranger were nearby. I would take time to soothe them, to reassure them that all was well. Now, it is one thing for children to be afraid of strangers, upset by anyone different. That's understandable. For adults, though? What makes it so hard for us to grow up?

Guidelines for Small Group Discussion

In small group discussions, one can find many more perspectives than the few that are available to oneself alone. Staying curious about the views of others is useful! Each family presented in this book provides a chance to see multiple family dynamics in action. Here, it's important to stick to the overall goal of exploring the family stories of Scripture.

If you are interested in pursuing other goals, such as understanding your own family, or learning more about family systems theory, or talking with a coach about personal family stories, or researching your multigenerational background, or thinking about how these dynamics apply to congregations, there are many options. To get started on these goals, or to continue, perhaps, please see my website information below.

Chapter discussion format: Exploring the family stories of Scripture

1. Begin by sharing overall thoughts about the chapter.

   a. What stood out for you?

   b. Did anything surprise you?

2. Discuss the chapter as a whole.

   a. How do you look at the family problems in the chapter?

   b. What are the family's challenges?

   c. Did you find any new ways of seeing the story? What other perspectives would you add? Where do you have a different view?

3. Discuss the last entry of the chapter, the Seekers' Council. Case presentations, in which one therapist presents a challenging case and the others listen, comment, and raise more questions, are common in the counseling world. Here, the Council discussions are set up to invite readers to sit alongside the therapists and consider these biblical families. Some starter questions are below—you may have many more!

   a. Did the family chart make a difference in how you saw the family?

   b. How would you respond to the concerns and questions section? What questions would you ask the presenter? Where would you see things differently from the presenter?

   c. Under the comments by topic, which topics seem most important? Which questions were the most interesting? How would you answer them?

4. Closing

   a. Spend a few minutes thinking, or perhaps writing, about the chapter. What new insights do you have into the Scripture?

   b. Share, in thirty seconds or less, your key thought.

In closing

Thank you for your interest in my work. More information about family systems thinking and its integration with Scripture and congregational life, including recommendations for books, websites, YouTube videos, ways of exploring your own family, and options for finding a family coach is available at my website, https://barbaralaymon.com. Please visit me there!